THE
SUPERPOWERS
AND THE
MIDDLE EAST

Contemporary Issues in the Middle East

ALAN R. TAYLOR

THE
SUPERPOWERS
AND THE
MIDDLE EAST

SYRACUSE UNIVERSITY PRESS

First Edition 1991
91 92 93 94 95 96 97 98 99   6 5 4 3 2 1

The paper used in this publication meets the minimum
requirements of American National Standard for imforma-
tion Sciences—Permanence of Paper for Printed Library
Materials, ANSI Z39.48-1984.∞™

LIBRARY OF CONGRESS CATALOGING-IN-PUBLICATION DATA
Taylor, Alan R.
    The superpowers and the Middle East/Alan R. Taylor.—1st ed.
    p.   cm.—(Contemporary issues in the Middle East)
Includes bibliographical references and index.
    ISBN 0-8156-2542-1 (cloth).—ISBN 0-8156-2543-x (paper)
    1. Middle East—Foreign relations—United States.   2. United States—
Foreign relations—Middle East.   3. Middle East—Foreign relations—
Soviet Union.   4. Soviet Union—Foreign relations—Middle East.
5. United States—Foreign relations—1945–   I. Title.   II. Series.
DS63.2.5T39   1991
327.56073—dc20   91-7639

To my brother, Robert,
who was the first to interest me
in the Middle East

Alan R. Taylor is a professor of Middle East
studies at the American University's School of
International Service in Washington, D.C. He is
the author of *The Arab Balance of Power* (Syracuse
University Press), *The Islamic Question in Middle
East Politics*, *Prelude to Israel: An Analysis of
Zionist Diplomacy, 1897–1947*, and *The Zionist
Mind: The Origins and Development of Zionist
Thought*.

For, said he [the Principal Secretary of Lilliput],
as flourishing a condition as we appear to be in
to foreigners, we labour under two mighty evils;
a violent faction home, and the danger of an
invasion by a most potent enemy from abroad
[Blefuscu] . . . I [Gulliver] desired the secretary
to present my humble duty to the emperor, and
to let him know, that I thought it would not
become me, who was a foreigner, to interfere
with parties; but I was ready; with the hazard of
my life, to defend his person and state against
all invaders.

JONATHAN SWIFT, *Gulliver's Travels*

CONTENTS

PREFACE

In Jonathan Swift's classic, *Gulliver's Travels*, the hero's first visit is to Lilliput, where the inhabitants are barely six inches tall. Though the author uses this fantasy to satirize eighteenth-century European politics, it can be reinterpreted to have symbolic meaning in a number of modern contexts. Not the least of these is the subject of this book: the superpower rivalry in the Middle East.

Gulliver is washed ashore on the island of Lilliput after being shipwrecked. On regaining consciousness, he finds himself a captive of the Lilliputians, bound by a multitude of strings they had attached to him. An involved relationship with the miniature people follows, one not unlike the present-day superpower relationship with the Middle Eastern states.

Gulliver actually has the power to free himself and utterly destroy the Lilliputians, but decides instead to be deferential and accommodating. His captors accordingly treat him with suspicion and condescension. They initially consider putting him to death with poisoned arrows, but then decide in favor of confiscating his belongings and imposing strict conditions on his behavior. While he is in the process of signing various documents agreeing to their demands, he is astonished to learn that most of their domestic strife concerns absurd debates over the use of high and low heels and whether boiled eggs should be opened at the small or large end. He also discovers that they are at war with the rival empire of Blefuscu, a conflict so bitter that the Lilliputian government is intent on virtually enslaving the entire enemy population.

Finally, Gulliver is allowed to move about freely, but is obliged to assist them in their struggle against the rival empire of Blefuscu, though he declines to help subjugate its people. Despite his cordiality and cooperation, however, a clique that had been ill-disposed toward Gulliver from the beginning succeeds in carrying out a successful conspiracy against him. The emperor of Lilliput is convinced by the conspirators that the giant stranger sympathizes with the Big-Endian heresy in the egg controversy and that he has been a traitor in refusing to help subjugate Blefuscu. He is therefore condemned to be blinded. On learning of this, Gulliver escapes to Blefuscu, where he is eventually granted permission to return to his own country.

The United States and the Soviet Union have been intense rivals in the Middle East since the end of World War II. They have actively sought to establish patron-client relationships with the indigenous states and become involved in regional politics and disputes. Like Gulliver in Lilliput, they have been confronted with ideologies and controversies they do not fully understand, and often their alignments with local powers have proved unreliable or disappointing.

The major theme of this book is that despite the vastly superior strength of the United States and the Soviet Union, both countries have had difficulty in dealing advantageously with their Middle Eastern clients and in protecting their respective interests in the area. The principal reason for this is that their approach has been global rather than regional, that they have been so involved in their rivalry with each other that they have not adequately assessed the political, social, and psychological dynamics of the Middle East itself. In this sense, they have indeed been "giants in Lilliput," strong but often confused and gullible actors in a volatile region they consider important to their interests but find difficult to control. Only very recently has this pattern of interaction begun to change significantly.

The methodology of this study is based on historical analysis, concentrating on the interaction between superpower Middle East policy and the social and political forces that determine behavior within the area. The emphasis is on developing an interpretation of the *actual* options and constraints confronting the United States and the Soviet Union.

The final alterations in the manuscript were made during the Gulf crisis and the early stages of the war that followed. Every attempt was made to bring the book up to date as much as possible, and to draw conclusions that would not be significantly changed by the course of future events.

Transliteration conforms to popular usage in the case of common names and expressions, and to standard professional usage otherwise. Diacritical marks and nonphonetic endings have, however, been eliminated.

I thank my friend Frank Versaci and my graduate assistants Yehuda Lukacs, Erika Alin, Francesco Alberti, and Sarah Morris for their suggestions and their help in preparing the manuscript for publication. I am also indebted to professor Dan Tschirgi of the American University in Cairo for pointing out ways to improve the manuscript.

ALAN R. TAYLOR

March 1991

THE
SUPERPOWERS
AND THE
MIDDLE EAST

1   LEGACIES

OLLOWING World War II, a new political structure was established in the international order. Its principal characteristic was the emergence of the United States and the Soviet Union as the dominant "superpowers" in a new global balance that replaced the old European "great power" system up to the late 1980s. Another important development was the rapid decolonization of Asian and African countries that had been under Western control for an extended period, in some cases for centuries. The combination of these two fundamental changes created a pattern of highly diversified interaction between the superpowers and the liberated Third World states.

A number of paradoxes underlay the encounter, occasionally producing bizarre episodes. The first is that although the superpowers disassociated themselves from the undisguised imperialism of the nineteenth-century European powers and the Russian Empire, they were nevertheless influenced in their behavior by this earlier tradition. The United States was never involved in the Western colonization of Asia and Africa, and the Soviet Union consciously rejected Tsarist empire-building. Both also claimed to represent loftier ideals such as "the world must be made safe for democracy," in the words of Woodrow Wilson,[1] and the self-proclaimed Soviet commitment to supporting all "progressive" forces in the world.[2]

Yet despite the self-images and ideological predilections involved, the United States and the Soviet Union were faced with

1. William Appleman Williams, *The Tragedy of American Diplomacy* (New York: Dell, 1962), p. 63.
2. Fred Halliday, *Soviet Policy in the Arc of Crisis* (Washington, D.C.: Institute for Policy Studies, 1981), p. 28.

international political exigencies not unlike those their forerunners had to confront. The international system was still based on
the structural balance of power. It was also still competitive and
often ruthless. Without subscribing to theories of historical de-
terminism, therefore, it is possible to say that today's superpowers have inherited certain legacies passed on to them by
previous political traditions that they do not regard as natural
sources of what they represent, but that they have nonetheless
perpetuated in certain respects under different auspices and
justifications.

The liberated Asian-African countries, for their part, have had
mixed attitudes and feelings about their relationship with the
new superpowers. In the case of the Middle East, the United
States enjoyed a relatively favorable reputation up to the end
of World War II because of its nonimperialist past. The Soviet
Union was regarded at the time of its establishment in 1917 as
having broken with the Tsarist imperial tradition, but its retention of the Caucasian and Central Asian provinces by force in the
following few years left some doubt about its actual intentions.
The attempted Soviet intrusion into the Northern Tier of the
Middle East in the immediate post–World War II period deep-
ened these concerns.

In the decades after 1945, the Middle Eastern states constantly
altered their policies toward the superpowers. They were forced
to determine the reliability of professed American and Soviet
idealism and to weigh the pragmatic advantages of alignment
with one or the other, or of a neutralism that offered possibilities
of a limited relationship with both. They also had to keep careful
track of the major tactical moves of the superpowers as they
acted out their international rivalry without much regard for
how lesser states might get hurt in the process. A lesson of
history that had not been forgotten was that an intense rivalry
had taken place in an earlier but still relatively recent period
between the forerunners of these new superpowers. In that case
the outcome was catastrophic for the indigenous societies and

peoples, since it had led to the massive intrusion of imperial Russia and the European great powers and the partition of almost the entire region among them. Though there may not have been an anticipation that the past would repeat itself, there were enough parallels between the old situation and the new to warrant extreme caution by the Middle Eastern states in their various dealings with the United States and the Soviet Union.

Western Colonization of the Middle East

The transformation of Western thought and culture produced by the Renaissance, one of the major developments in the history of mankind according to C. E. Black,[3] established a new system of relationships between Europe and the Afro-Asian world. The term "Renaissance" is a very generalized way of referring to what was more accurately the secular revolution that unfolded in western and central Europe roughly between the fourteenth and seventeenth centuries. The radical change in perceptions and values that this revolution entailed was multifaceted. Religion gradually ceased to occupy the center of European institutional life, and the increasing influence of empiricism and inductive science completely altered traditional views of man and reality. The dominant focus of concern became temporal human needs, producing a new emphasis on utility.

Utilitarianism manifested itself in a variety of ways. The obsolescence of feudalism led to a political revolution in which the interests of emerging nation states under monarchical leadership became paramount. The idea of patriotism embraced by the membership of Europe's ethnolinguistic groups replaced the old feudal bonds of fealty, and gave rise to collective endeavors that unleashed the full potential of the human resources residing in each self-designated national community. The power generated by this phenomenon was greatly enhanced by the application of

3. C. E. Black, *The Dynamics of Modernization: A Study in Comparative History* (New York: Harper and Row, 1966), p. 4.

the scientific revolution to all fields of technology, especially those related to productivity, warfare, and navigation. United by a new sense of identity and dedication to common goals and aspirations, the emerging Western nationalities came to form a dynamic state system that was destined to challenge and radically change the world.

Modern Europe was transformed by its own secular revolution into a social culture that was at the same time given over to utilitarian values and methodology, powerful because of its sociopolitical integration and advanced technology, adventurous on account of its newly acquired mobility, and acquisitive often to the point of aggressiveness. As the Europeans moved into the world with their greatly improved ability to travel long distances by sea, they came into closer contact than ever before with the cultures of Asia, Africa, and the Americas. What they found in all cases were societies that were either relatively primitive by Western standards or in a stage of civilizational decline that made them vulnerable to external intrusion and colonization. Even the neighboring Ottoman Empire, only recently an extremely powerful state that had threatened Europe itself, was less and less capable of coping with the Western challenge.

This led to a system of relationships in which the Europeans became involved in a comprehensive and rampant colonization of virtually the entire non-Western world over a period of centuries. An important element in this process was the attitude of the conquerors toward the indigenous populations of the acquired territories. The question of rights was almost never taken into consideration; the inhabitants of what later became known as the Third World were essentially dehumanized in the minds of the colonizers. The exploitation, displacement, and even extermination of these peoples was explained or excused as part of a civilizing role the West had assumed—a *"mission civilisatrice"* involving a "white man's burden."

The native "Indian" populations of the Americas were completely displaced and destroyed as viable cultures, except for preserved remnants. The penetration of Africa initially gave rise to a thriving slave trade, and then to the partition of the entire continent except for Ethiopia. Much of Asia was either brought under direct control or penetrated by Europeans, who indirectly manipulated economic and political affairs to their advantage. Throughout the process, the indigenous peoples were treated with condescension and contempt. Expressions such as Wogs for the Egyptians and Fuzzy Wuzzies for the Sudanese reflected the profound disrespect of the Europeans for the peoples they had colonized. The deep-rootedness of these attitudes is borne out by the continuation of such pejoratives in Western reference to non-Westerners, labels like "ragheads" and "gooks."

Western imperialists regarded and treated the inhabitants of the Third World as inferior. They had little respect for the cultures of the indigenous peoples and almost no sense of guilt over the way their human and physical resources were exploited. The overall process was insensitive at best and cruel at worst. What is of principal concern here is the changing pattern of relationships that developed as the non-Western reaction to Western intrusions gained momentum and viability. First, however, it is important to examine Western imperialism as it unfolded in the Middle East.

Western imperialism in the Middle East took the form of political and economic intrusion into the Ottoman Empire, Iran, Afghanistan, and the Arab sheikhdoms of the Persian Gulf and southern Arabia. A corresponding Russian intervention in the Caucasus and Turkestan took place simultaneously. In the Western case, the principal actors were the Austrian Empire, Great Britain, France, and Italy, each of which had its own particular reasons for seeking advantages in the Middle East and North Africa. Austria wanted to compensate for its losses in central Europe after the Thirty Years War and saw expansion to the east at the expense of the Ottoman Empire as a natural course of action. Great Britain had a special interest in preserving unrestricted access to India, and developed a policy of protecting the Ottoman Empire, especially from Russia, and making it a kind of dependency. France, which had always considered the Mediterranean important to its strategic, political, and economic position in the world, sought to maintain a degree of strength and influence in the Middle East and North Africa. Italy eventually developed a similar attitude toward Mediterranean affairs and became active in the imperialist expansion into the Middle East in the latter part of the nineteenth century.

The coincidence of these motives and the decline of the Ottoman Empire and surrounding Middle Eastern states gave rise to the "Eastern Question," the question of how the European powers, already competitive with regard to each other, were going to fill the power vacuum engendered by the disintegration of political viability in the Middle East. As in all cases of Western imperialism, there was absolutely no consideration of the adverse consequences the intrusion might bring to the indigenous peoples, no thought that they might have rights that were being violated. The only preoccupation of the powers involved was their own options and constraints in relative terms. Theirs was a totally amoral and pragmatic orientation based on a realistic appraisal of the power structure.

As L. Carl Brown has noted, there is no general agreement on when the Eastern Question began.[4] Though the term was not used until the nineteenth century, the most logical date is 1699. It was in that year that the Treaty of Carlowitz concluded a prolonged war between the Ottoman Empire and the European alliance that had been formed to combat the second siege of Vienna in 1683. The war demonstrated the military superiority of the West, despite subsequent periodic Ottoman victories, and a new chapter in Ottoman-European relations had been permanently opened.

4. . L. Carl Brown, *International Politics and the Middle East: Old Rules, Dangerous Game* (Princeton, NJ: Princeton University Press, 1984), pp. 21–30.

The Treaty of Carlowitz marked the beginning of Western encroachment on Ottoman territory. The larger part of Hungary that had been under Ottoman sovereignty, Transylvania, and parts of Slovenia and Croatia were transferred to Austria, an enormous concession forced on the Sublime Porte (Ottoman government). Henceforth the European powers regarded the Ottoman Empire as a declining imperium, increasingly vulnerable to Western intrusion and control. As "the sick man of Europe" it came to be thought of as spoils to be divided in some way by the competing states in the imperialist power game.

The history of the Eastern Question has been covered in concise form and in detail elsewhere.[5] The principal concern here is to analyze the patterns that the intrusion assumed as the process gathered momentum and intensity. Of particular interest are the methods of the Europeans and the attitudes that developed on all sides in what L. Carl Brown has called the "diplomatic culture"[6] of the Eastern Question.

The general character of the Eastern Question as an international system was considerably changed by the Russian expansion into Ottoman territory during the reign of Catherine the Great (1762–96) and by the adventures of Napoleon in the area. The policies of these two renowned rulers brought a century of territorial incursion to its pinnacle, and introduced concepts of intervention and control that marked the beginning of comprehensive colonization and the restriction or termination of indigenous rights of sovereignty in the Middle East. The Treaty of Kutchuk Kainardji (1774), which will be examined in greater detail later, not only made Russia a Black Sea power but established loosely defined rights of Russian intervention in Ottoman affairs on behalf of Christians. This kind of special prerogative

5. See George Lenczowski, *The Middle East in World Affairs,* 4th edition (Ithaca, NY: Cornell University Press, 1980), pp. 27–51; J. A. R. Marriott, *The Eastern Question: An Historical Study in European Diplomacy* (Oxford: Oxford University Press, 1940); M. S. Anderson, *The Eastern Question, 1774–1923: A Study in International Relations* (New York: St. Martin's Press, 1966).

6. Brown, p. 21.

was to be asserted by various powers throughout the subsequent history of the classical Eastern Question and into the years of Soviet-American rivalry in the area. Napoleon's invasion of Egypt in 1798, though not ultimately successful in a military or political sense, initiated a kind of cultural penetration that became increasingly important in the succeeding decades and up to the present. From that point forward, Middle Eastern political leaders were drawn with ever stronger attraction to Western models in search of solutions to the challenges confronting their own societies. This created the psychological climate that shaped the diplomatic culture of European–Middle Eastern interaction.

The Eastern Question was overshadowed by the dramatic events of the Napoleonic wars. The major significant development produced by this period was the complete subordination of regional politics to the rivalries of the Western state system. This engendered a manipulative posture among the Europeans that manifested itself in a series of imposed settlements in the Middle East after the Congress of Vienna in 1815.

The Greek uprising in the 1820s led to European intervention and the establishment of a small independent Greek kingdom in 1830. The attempts of the ambitious Albanian governor of Egypt, Muhammad Ali, to overthrow the Ottoman Empire brought about another Western intervention and subsequent settlement. A sectarian civil war in Lebanon in 1860 concerned the Europeans to the point that a French task force was dispatched to the area. A few years later, a new system of government for Lebanon based on a balance of sectarian interests was imposed on the Ottoman rulers. Finally, an uprising in the Balkans in 1875 brought all the rivalries of the Eastern Question to the surface, producing an international crisis. So many interests were involved that a comprehensive settlement was required. The Congress of Berlin, which was convened in 1878 for this purpose, imposed a completely new order in the Balkans, establishing independent states without reference to Ottoman interests. This violation of sovereignty opened a new phase of the Eastern Question in which the dominant theme was partition of the Middle East.

The relentlessness and rapidity with which the European powers took over virtually the entire Middle East between the Congress of Berlin and World War I is staggering. Footholds had already been established by France in Algeria and by Great Britain in the Persian Gulf and south Arabia before 1878. But the momentum of these earlier incursions increased dramatically afterwards. France occupied Tunisia in 1881, and Great Britain took over Egypt the following year. These events initiated a chain of agreements among the various actors in the European state system to partition the Middle East in conjunction with the alliances they were forming with each other. Eventually, Iran and Afghanistan were divided into Russian and British zones of influence in 1907, Italy was allowed to occupy Libya in 1911, and France established control of Morocco in 1912. The new German Empire, created in 1871, also became involved in the late nineteenth century, and drew the Ottoman imperium into its alliance system. The Fertile Crescent, which remained under Ottoman rule, was placed under British and French administrative jurisdiction after World War I as part of the mandate system established in former colonies of the defeated powers. The only areas to escape this rampant imperialism were central Arabia and Yemen. The Eastern Question had run its full course.

The diplomatic culture that Brown sees as an important product of European–Middle Eastern interaction in recent centuries is based on corresponding attitudes developed by both sides. From the Western perspective, the Middle East represented a declining civilization, one whose peoples and governments were inept and incapable of dealing effectively with reality and whose cultures and institutions were not to be taken seriously. The West had not only a right to exploit the area politically and economically, but a duty to enrich it with its own superior culture.

The Middle Eastern reaction to this condescension and to the intrusiveness that accompanied it was ambivalent. Because of the area's inability to take effective counteraction, its instinctive responses—anger and resentment—were transformed into either obsequiousness or a determination to imitate Western techniques and methods as a means of combating European aggressiveness. This led to the emergence of classic Middle Eastern behavioral types with respect to the "Western question": the docile collaborator and the nationalist-liberationist agitator. A third type also began to appear in the form of the Islamic revivalist.

The diplomatic culture of the Eastern Question was, however, constantly changing, especially as imperialism began to be eclipsed after World War I. The liberation process brought many new factors into what had been a relatively simple equation. Political and economic power became diversified, and though the West maintained military superiority, it had to cope with the constraints imposed by indigenous forces representing regional interests. This shift in the structure of the Eastern Question required a change in perception and approach on the part of the West that was often not forthcoming. The inability of the Europeans and Americans to shape Middle East policy in terms of what was happening on the ground in the area became the greatest stumbling block in their search to protect their interests there.

The kind of relationship the West had with the Middle East in the nineteenth century does not exist anymore. There is a continuity of the external rivalries for power and influence in the region, but indigenous social and political forces now have to be taken into account. As the superpower that inherited the legacy of Western intervention in the Middle East, the United States had the responsibility, forced on it by historical circumstance, of analyzing the actual forces at work in the area and developing an appropriate policy within that context. Failure to do so had a deleterious effect on Western interests, and created disadvantages for the U.S. in its competition with the Soviet Union. Accurate perception of regional dynamics is equally important in the post–Cold War era of the 1990s and beyond.

The Imperial Russian Drive to the South

The Russian relationship with the Middle East stems from different circumstances. The Muscovite state of which Peter the Great (1689–1725) became ruler at the end of the seventeenth century was severely restricted in terms of its future development by the traditional threat to its security posed by the Latin West, and by the isolation from the world caused by its lack of access to the necessary sea lanes. Absorbed by these problems, Peter devoted his life to modernizing Russia so that it could compete with the West, and to bringing the country out of isolation by expansion to the Baltic and Black Seas. The drive to the south was into the Middle East, and initiated a new relationship between Russia and this neighboring area.

Peter joined the European alliance against the Ottoman Empire and captured the port of Azov at the northeastern tip of the Sea of Azov, which, though a temporary conquest, marked the beginning of an expanding Russian presence on the Black Sea. This initiated an extensive Russian incursion into the Middle East that has continued to the present.

By the end of Catherine's reign, the Russian Empire was firmly entrenched on the northern shores of the Black Sea. Moreover, Russia interpreted the Treaty of Kutchuk Kainardji as giving it a right to intervene in Ottoman internal affairs on behalf of at least the Orthodox Christians living in Ottoman territory. Interventions of various sorts soon brought Russia into direct and often intense competition with the European powers and made it a central actor in the Eastern Question.

After the Napoleonic wars, Russian Middle East strategy was concentrated on three principal objectives. The first was to extend as much as possible the assumed protectorate over Ottoman Christians. The second was to gain special rights of passage through the Turkish Straits in order to obtain full access to the warm waters of the Mediterranean. The final and most ambitious objective was to incorporate the Caucasus and Turkestan into the Russian Empire, at the expense of Iran and the Ottoman imperium in the first case and of the independent Central Asian Muslim principalities in the second. The underlying goal of these policies was to encircle the Black and Caspian Seas and convert the Ottoman Empire, Iran, and Afghanistan into dependencies or zones of dominant influence.

Russia used the Greek insurrection of the 1820s to press its claim to a protectorate over the Orthodox Christians of the Ottoman Empire and to extend its position on the eastern shores of the Black Sea. A Russo-Turkish war that began in 1828 ended with the Treaty of Adrianople of 1829, which confirmed a Russian protectorate over the Danubian principalities of Rumania and transferred portions of the western Caucasus to Russia. This treaty, comparable in importance to Kutchuk Kainardji, marked a significant advance of Russian interests in the Eastern Question, and was followed by even bolder moves.

The Muhammad Ali episode of the 1830s, which threatened to bring the vulnerable Ottoman Empire under the control of the talented and ambitious governor of Egypt, led to a Russian intervention ostensibly to assist the beleaguered Ottoman sultan. This resulted in the Treaty of Unkiar Skelessi in 1833. On the surface it was a mutual defense agreement, but in secret clauses it gave Russia special rights over the Straits in time of war and created a kind of Russian protectorate over the Ottoman Empire. Great Britain and other powers involved in the Eastern Question were deeply concerned by this turn of events, and they took advantage of the general European intervention in 1839 to restore the previous balance of interests. The Treaty of London in 1840 and the Convention of the Straits in 1841 resolved the Turkish-Egyptian dispute and terminated Russia's privileged position in the strategic waterway.

Subsequent Russian efforts to reach an accord with Great

Britain on a mutually agreeable partition of the Ottoman Empire were unfruitful, and Russian policy underwent a series of setbacks in the following three decades. The most serious reverse was in connection with the Crimean War. A dispute over Orthodox and Roman Catholic privileges in the holy places of Palestine was expanded to encompass the broader and more sensitive issue of Russian rights in the Ottoman Empire in general. The parties were unable to resolve this delicate question, and the Russo-Turkish war that broke out in 1853 became the Crimean War in 1854, with Great Britain, France, and the Italian Kingdom of Sardinia siding with the Ottoman Empire against Russia. The ultimate victory of the allied countries led to the Treaty of Paris in 1856, which canceled many of Russia's previous gains. The Black Sea was neutralized and the idea of a Russian protectorate over Ottoman Christians was rejected, effectively nullifying those aspects of the Treaties of Kutchuk Kainardji and Adrianople which the Russians had used to forward their claims.

In 1871 Russia succeeded in revoking the Black Sea clauses of the Treaty of Paris, a move designed to regain some initiative in the Middle East. This was followed by the Balkan uprising of 1875 and a new heated episode in the history of the Eastern Question. Following intricate diplomatic maneuvers, Russia was given a conditional right to intervene on behalf of the Balkan insurgents, many of whom were ethnically Slavic or religiously Orthodox or both. The Russo-Turkish war of 1877–78 and a predictable Russian victory followed. In contravention of an agreement with Austria, Russia concluded the Treaty of San Stefano with the Ottoman Empire, creating an abnormally large Bulgaria as a virtual Russian dependency. This was, of course, rejected by the European powers, and at the Congress of Berlin later in 1878 a more equitable pan-European dispensation of the Balkans was agreed upon.

Despite these setbacks in the Eastern Question, Russia had managed to establish control over approximately half of the Black Sea coastline and to enjoy at least equal access to the

Turkish Straits. Also, during the turbulent decades of rivalry over the Ottoman Empire, it had been engaged in another competition—this one with Great Britain alone—over the eastern Caucasus, Turkestan, Iran, and Afghanistan. Anglo-Russian interaction in these areas was referred to either as the Central Asian Question, the Middle Eastern Question, or the "Great Game." The stakes were high. Russia sought access to the Indian Ocean, Great Britain a protected imperial lifeline to India, aims that were clearly incompatible.

The rivalry began in the early nineteenth century, when British envoys from India began contracting alliances with the Persian court. During the same period, a Russian dispute with Persia led to war and the Treaty of Gulistan in 1813, through which the eastern and southern Caucasus became part of the Russian Empire and Russian naval domination of the Caspian Sea was established. This was complemented by the later moves into the western Caucasus at the expense of the Ottoman Empire. The Treaty of Turkomanchai in 1828 ended another Russo-Persian war, and together with the Russo-Turkish Treaty of Adrianople the following year completed the Russian annexation of the entire Caucasus. It is seldom recognized that the conquest of this area represents the incorporation into the Russian Empire of a whole component region of the Middle East, a remarkable and significant achievement.

Beginning in the 1830s, the Great Game focused on the rest of Iran and on Afghanistan, as well as on the vast region of Turkestan directly to the north. An incredible saga of intrigue, clandestine operations, and warfare took place over the following several decades. Russian agents promoted and collaborated with a Persian scheme to conquer and incorporate the western Afghan city of Herat, a move designed to compensate Persia for her earlier losses to Russia in the Caucasus, but the project ultimately ended in failure. Despite several minor wars involving Great Britain, Persia, and Afghanistan, the only major change in the Iranian Plateau area in the nineteenth century was the emergence of an Afghan state.

Meanwhile, Russia began to move into Turkestan. In deliberate and carefully planned military campaigns against the independent Khanates of Bukhara, Khiva, and Kokand in 1868, 1873, and 1876, respectively, Russia conquered these states and incorporated them into the Russian Empire. The Turkoman territory just to the south was also taken in the early 1880s, culminating in the capture of Merv in 1884. This completed the Russian annexation of yet another component region of the Middle East.

The dramatic Russian drive to the south in Trans-Caspia brought on a series of Anglo-Russian crises in the mid-1880s and mid-1890s. War was avoided by an agreement delimiting the northern borders of Afghanistan. Great Britain and Russia then moved toward a more general accord in Central Asia; the result was in the Anglo-Russian Agreement of 1907, in which the two empires partitioned Iran and Afghanistan between themselves. Northern Iran was recognized as a Russian sphere, southern Iran and Afghanistan as a British sphere. This agreement formed part of the overall partition of the Middle East area mentioned earlier.

There were a number of reasons for the Russian expansion into the Middle East. One was to break out of the isolation that had kept the country distant from most of the world before the reign of Peter. This isolation had not only made Russia traditionally vulnerable to attack from the hostile West, but also prevented it from participating in the secular revolution that had transformed the rest of Europe. Peter's policies of expansion to the Baltic and Black Seas and modernization along Western lines were essential to the survival of Russia in an increasingly mobile and competitive world.

Another reason for the Russian move toward the adjacent Middle East area was the area's significant Orthodox and Slavic populations. The Russians had always considered themselves the protectors of Orthodox Christians in the Holy Land and other parts of the Middle East, as well as those in the Balkans and Rumania. During the second half of the nineteenth century, they also developed a strong sense of identity with and protective responsibility for the Southern Slavs of the Balkan Peninsula because of the powerful pan-Slav movement that had captured the popular imagination of the country. At a time when ethnic nationality was strongly emphasized, they were highly conscious of what they perceived as an emerging struggle between the Germanic and Slavic ethnic groups for the mastery of Europe and areas beyond.[7]

Once actively involved in the Middle East, the Russians began to look at it as a primary security region. They became extremely aware of its location on Russia's southern periphery and of the importance of maintaining access to the warm water sea routes. In strategic terms, these matters were as important to them as the preoccupation with preserving the imperial lifeline to India was to Great Britain.

One other consideration is difficult to substantiate but was put forward rather convincingly by the British historian Arnold Toynbee, namely a state's compulsion to expand for its own sake without necessary regard for expansion's more specific advantages.[8] Toynbee held that civilizations tend to expand almost automatically as their cultural traditions go into decline, as a sort of compensation for that decline. Thus the Roman Empire followed the decline of Hellenic civilization. Whether or not this theory is valid, it is evident that the Muscovite state expanded into a vast empire as traditional post-Byzantine Russian culture went into decline, and that as Russia Westernized, its rulers became increasingly adamant about expansion and protecting the security of their ever more extensive domains.

Russian empire-building, including the intrusion into the Middle East, differed in a substantial way from Western imperialism. Whereas the British, French, and others built their colonies in far-flung regions and kept the indigenous peoples as

7. S. V. Utechin, *Russian Political Thought: A Concise History* (New York: Praeger, 1963), pp. 86–87; Thomas Garrigue Masaryk, *The Spirit of Russia: Studies in History, Literature and Philosophy*, 2 vols., translated by Eden and Cedar Paul (London: Allen & Unwin, 1919), I, 291–93.

8. Arnold J. Toynbee, *A Study of History*, 10 vols. (London: Oxford University Press, 1954), VII, 1–6, 31–40.

inferior subjects without equal rights, the Russians simply expanded into adjacent areas, incorporating them into an always geographically contiguous empire while granting citizenship to their inhabitants.

There was, however, a subtle aspect of this Russian practice that was never fully examined or analyzed in terms of its ultimate consequences. This was the fact that the Russian Empire, unlike the Muscovite state, was a multinational, multiethnic, multilinguistic pluralistic entity. Though the Russians may not have treated the non-Russian nationalities with the same condescension as the British did the colonized peoples under their rule, there was never any question that the dominant element in their empire was the Russian one. Hence, when nationalism spread to the Third World and caught on among the non-Russian nationalities in the late nineteenth century, the Russian state had no effective way of dealing with this new phenomenon. The British and French simply tried to keep it in check, and then let go when it got out of control. The imperial Russian government ceased to exist before it had to deal seriously with this question; but its Soviet successors had to cope with the problem from their earliest days in power. During the civil war that followed the revolution, the non-Russian nationalities in the Caucasus and Turkestan tried to secede and were prevented from doing so by force.

As the Bolsheviks consolidated power, all forms of nonconformity were dealt with ruthlessly and opposition of any kind was effectively eliminated. Yet the Soviet Union has never satisfactorily resolved the problem of the non-Russian nationalities. Just as the relationship between the West and the Middle East is not the same as it was in the nineteenth century, so the relationship between the dominant Russian component of the Soviet Union and the non-Russian nationalities is not the same as it was under the Tsars or Stalin. In the Middle Eastern region the social and political forces of the country's Caucasian and Turkestan components have to be taken into account, a fact particularly evident in the recent Armenian-Azerbaijani controversy. Similarly, as the Soviet Union looks for advantages in the Middle East beyond its borders, it has to reckon with the social and political forces there as well.

Reincarnation of an Old Rivalry

World War I and the Russian Revolution significantly altered the system of relationships that had characterized the Eastern Question for over two centuries, though the change was not always obvious. The new regime in Russia, itself in a process of transition, renounced all Tsarist schemes for the partition of the Middle East but steadfastly held onto those components of the area that had been incorporated into the old Russian Empire. The Western colonial powers not only made no move to relinquish their existing dependencies, but sought to divide among themselves much of Anatolia and the Fertile Crescent. All that came of this endeavor was the establishment of British and French mandates in Greater Syria and Mesopotamia.

As we now know the underlying reality was that the age of imperialism was coming to a close and giving way to a new dispensation in which African and Asian liberation movements were to play an increasingly active role. Dramatic changes had already occurred: the dismantling of the German, Austrian, and Ottoman Empires as well as the nominal disappearance of the Tsarist imperium. Yet the full implication of African and Asian nationalism was still an enigma. A transitional period ensued, in which the foundations of a very different world order were being laid. The emerging superpowers and the new Third World states were to be key actors in this order, while the nations of western and central Europe groped for a cooperative system that would make them a force to be reckoned with in international politics.

During the interwar period, the United States and the Soviet Union disassociated themselves from the imperialist traditions of the West and the Tsarist empire and concentrated on their internal problems and development. The U.S. took a consciously isolationist attitude toward a world it did not want to become involved in, and the Soviet Union abandoned the role of revolutionary vanguard of the working class in favor of the Stalinist doctrine of building socialism in one country. Its top priority was to catch up with a West it feared and considered a dangerous threat to its survival. Both countries operated within their own frames of reference, with secondary though cautious regard for the new conflagration that was emerging in the context of European affairs.

When the war came, they both stayed out. The United States, though sympathizing with the Western allies, tried to remain aloof from the conflict. The Soviet Union, feeling unprepared for a confrontation with Germany, allowed itself to be drawn into an uneasy and tenuous alliance with Hitler. This incidentally, but not insignificantly, had its advantages in terms of the U.S.S.R.'s enhanced position vis-à-vis the states lying between its borders and those of the Third Reich. It was a foreview of the later Russian expansion into eastern Europe. Then in 1941, the Soviet Union and the United States were drawn into World War II, inaugurating what was to be a transformed international structure in which they became the two dominant powers.

The war also marked the beginning of a new situation in the Middle East. Iran was occupied by Great Britain and the Soviet Union after Hitler's invasion of Russia. Much of northern Africa was the scene of a prolonged desert campaign. Syria and Lebanon fell under Free French control and subsequently achieved independence. Palestine became unsettled because of the ardent Zionist determination to establish a Jewish state. Turkey maintained an uneasy neutrality, always fearful of a potential German conquest. And internally, new political forces threatening relatively radical change drifted to the surface. All of the elements that were to make the area volatile and politically unstable after 1945 had already appeared during the great struggle against the Third Reich.

In the immediate postwar period, the dominant themes of the

revised international structure of the Middle East and of world politics became quickly apparent. The European powers, exhausted by the war, began the gradual process of decolonization. French control over Syria and Lebanon was terminated, and Great Britain started to dismantle its mandate in Palestine, not to mention its granting of independence to India. The age of imperialism was drawing to a close. Meanwhile, the Soviet Union, though itself spent by the grueling conflict that had just ended, began expanding on all its peripheries: into eastern Europe, the Middle East, and the Far East. The period of building socialism in one country ended dramatically, and the U.S.S.R. assumed the new role of superpower with remarkable forcefulness and resiliency. Similarly, the United States broke sharply with the tradition of isolationism, becoming the other superpower and identifying itself as leader of the West and champion of the "free world."

The ideological disparity between the superpowers underscored the intense bipolarity of the new global system. At the same time, the decolonization process and the rise of nationalism had an issue-prone orientation. The combination of these characteristics filled the superpower–Middle East relationship with emotionally charged qualities that made it more dramatic and explosive than the old Eastern Question. Yet in many respects the United States and the Soviet Union, in their confrontation with each other in the Middle East, reincarnated the Anglo-Russian rivalry of the nineteenth century.

An attitude that ultimate national interests were at stake prevailed, making the Soviet-American competition more intense. Not only were ideological issues involved, but also the security of the U.S.S.R.'s southern periphery and of the U.S.'s extended defense line in the Mediterranean and Europe. For this reason the emphasis was on the priorities of the global approach, in which relative strategic advantage was the principal concern. As in the classical Eastern Question, the interests of the indigenous states and peoples were either seen as secondary or not taken into consideration at all.

Though the United States and the Soviet Union had officially renounced any links with Western and Tsarist imperialism, their behavior in dealing with Middle East politics was not unlike that of the great powers in the nineteenth century. Yet the considerably changed circumstances made this kind of continuity an anachronism. In the postwar world, unlike the earlier period, regional political and social forces had become a factor in the equation. This was the major paradox of Middle Eastern–superpower relations that made the rivalry more complicated and the area less stable and predictable.

2 CONFRONTATION

URING the first half of the nineteenth century, Alexis de Tocqueville predicted an eventual confrontation between Russia and America.[1] Looking to a post-European era of the future, he saw an inevitable clash of giant states that dwarfed Europe and were based on opposing social systems and political ideologies. It was an astonishing *avant-vue*, prophetic in its accuracy though perhaps somewhat limited in its analytical depth. Just such a clash became the dominant international reality in our world more than a hundred years later.

Two developments had to take place before the latent Russo-American rivalry could materialize. The first was for Russia to divest itself of the traditional Tsarist orientation that had made it part of the European state system and the colonization process. The second was for the United States to emerge from its self-imposed isolation and assume leadership of the Western world.

The Russian Revolution broke with the past without dismantling the empire built by the Tsars. It paved the way to the eventual revitalization of Russia by destroying the archaic system of privilege and thereby facilitating a needed social integration. Though the Bolshevik regime perpetuated and even strengthened the preceding autocracy, it inadvertently made this very totalitarianism gradually unacceptable to a population it was slowly transforming through education and modernization. The combination of a continued imperial tradition in disguise, a

---

1. Alexis de Tocqueville, *Democracy in America*, edited by Henry Steele Commager and translated by Henry Reeve (New York: Oxford University Press, 1947), pp. 242–43.

radical change in social structure, forced modernization, and enormous reserves in human and natural resources was responsible for the emergence of the Soviet Union as a superpower in the twilight years of European imperialism.

The United States was drawn reluctantly into World War II, but once committed to the struggle it changed irrevocably. The profound alterations in the international power structure brought on by the war forced the U.S. to adopt a different view of its place in the world. A devastated Europe, unable to perpetuate its former global hegemony, was suddenly confronted by an amazingly resilient and assertive Soviet Union determined to establish its own dominance in the Eurasian heartland. The U.S.S.R. was also bent on resuming the communist leadership role it had relinquished earlier in order to build up and consolidate its own internal resources. For these reasons America found itself thrust into a position of protective leadership, not only for the West in general, but also for the kind of political-economic ideology of which it was the principal representative.

What had come to pass was a global political revolution in which the new superpowers were destined to act out an intense rivalry against the background of a changing Third World. Initially, however, their preoccupation concerned their relative strength with regard to each other.

The Cold War and the Middle East

The Cold War began with the resumption of Russian expansionism on the peripheries of the Soviet Union. Through agreement with the United States in particular, eastern Europe was placed in the Soviet sphere of influence. In the Far East, the U.S.S.R. gained the Kuriles and the southern half of Sakhalin Island from Japan, while actively assisting communist forces in China and establishing a dominant position in Outer Mongolia. In the Middle East, the Northern Tier came under intense Soviet pressure.

Greece, Turkey, and Iran were particular objects of Russian

maneuvering. The communist insurgents in northern Greece received Soviet aid in their attempt to take power. Turkey was given an ultimatum demanding the transfer of authority over the Straits to the Black Sea powers. In Iran, the Soviets tried to establish a puppet state in Azerbaijan. These events, combined with Soviet advances in eastern Europe and other parts of the world, alarmed the United States and played an important role in shaping the psychology of the Cold War. They also established the pattern of superpower interaction in the Middle East.

The dominant theme of the Soviet-American rivalry in the area has until recently been a relentless Russian attempt to construct a powerful security belt on the southwestern periphery of the Soviet Union, accompanied by an equally tenacious American determination to preserve under U.S. auspices the advantageous positions of strength built up previously by the Western colonial powers. Because of the strategic intercontinental location of the Middle East, its importance in Third World politics, and its increasingly vital petroleum resources, this competition became intense at an early stage and has remained so to the present. Not infrequently it has reached a point of dangerous sensitivity, close to straining superpower relations beyond acceptable limits.

Soviet strategy has evolved in phases, involving a combination of constants and variables. Among the constants is a practice derived from pre-Soviet Russian foreign policy, that of exerting pressure on peripheral areas when they are vulnerable and non-resistant but adopting a more accommodating stance when aggressive resistance is encountered. This was the way Tsarist governments dealt with the British in the Near and Middle East in the nineteenth century. Paradoxically, this aspect of Soviet policy was at the same time rigid and flexible: rigid in its unrelenting opportunism and flexible in its ability to adapt tactics to circumstances. This approach, however, was the major constant in the Soviet Union's approach to the Middle East.

The variables in Soviet Mideast strategy relate to shifting attitudes on how to operate most effectively in a volatile and often unpredictable area. The ideologically purist Marxist-Leninist line, which emphasized maximizing all opportunities to promote communist subversion and revolution, ran into difficulties in the early years of the Cold War. Subsequently, an adaptation of the more sophisticated "popular front" tactic, used in Europe before the war, proved more efficacious. The idea of the popular front was to establish an identity of interests between the Soviet Union and indigenous countries. Attempts to accommodate Middle East nationalism in a popular front were not always successful, but the Soviets did demonstrate a tactical ability to advance and protect their interests in an area where there was considerable resistance to external manipulation.

American strategy has also evolved in phases, though in a somewhat haphazard fashion. Initially, there was an awareness that the postwar international power structure demanded a far more active U.S. role in global politics than ever before. Added to this was a sense that the United States and its European allies had a political philosophy and way of life that must be defended in the context of a now formidable Soviet challenge. This polar view of the postwar world dominated American attitudes and became the primary consideration in the shaping of foreign policy in Washington.

The immediate U.S. concern in the Middle East was to contain Soviet expansionist moves by filling the power vacuum emerging from the incipient withdrawal of Great Britain and France from the area. When the British made it clear that they could no longer maintain support for Greece and Turkey,[2] the United States was forced by circumstances beyond its control to defend Western interests in the Mideast against the mounting Soviet threat. The idea of a commitment to fight for ultimate values on behalf of the West in a destabilized world became an obsession

2. George Lenczowski, *The Middle East in World Affairs*, 4th edition (Ithaca, NY: Cornell University Press, 1980), pp. 794–95.

that determined U.S. Middle East policy, often to the exclusion of other extremely important considerations. One of the major problems arising from this orientation was that American strategy often tended to be more reactive than innovative or carefully thought out. It even led some to question whether there really was a U.S. policy for the region in terms of defined aims and consistent behavior.

The Cold War in the Middle East unfolded in this context. All along, it was characterized by a series of moves and counter-moves designed to establish or preclude some perceived advantage. The initial Soviet intrusion into the Northern Tier injected a degree of urgency into the encounter at the outset. The United States reacted with a firm policy on Iran and the 1947 Truman Doctrine, which demonstrated American determination to hold the line against the Russians in Greece and Turkey. The Soviets, intent on reversing the traditional Western position of dominance in the Middle East south of the Caucasus and Turkestan, had to back down in this opening confrontation, and resorted instead to a policy of subversion and destabilization.

It was at this point that the Palestine question became the central issue in Middle East politics. In a reversal of their usual opposition to each other's position, the rival superpowers concurred on the partition of the British mandate into two independent states, one Jewish and one Arab. The reasons for their endorsement of partition were different, though some of their objectives were not completely clear. Soviet support was probably based on Moscow's desire to see British rule in Palestine ended as soon as possible so that different political forces would come into play there and in surrounding areas. This would open possibilities for the extension of Soviet influence. American support was based more on popular sympathy for the statehood project, which had been carefully cultivated by the Zionists during World War II, and on President Truman's interest in alleviating the Jewish refugee problem. In any event, the superpowers' mutual support for partition brought the Jewish state into existence and added a new element to the political equation in the Middle East. At a later date the Arab-Israeli conflict became an important focus of superpower friction.

The superpower rivalry gathered momentum in the 1950s. The United States finally succeeded in establishing a Middle East defense system through interlocking alliances among the Northern Tier countries. The Soviets' response was to pass over the Northern Tier and construct a counterveiling clientele system in the adjoining Arab sector. They were encouraged in this endeavor by the deteriorating relations between Washington and Cairo and the rising tension between Israel and Egypt. It was at this point that the Soviets began to resort to the popular front tactic they had employed in Europe in the 1930s. Emphasizing common Soviet-Arab interests, they expressed sympathy with Nasser's nationalist aims and support for the Arab side in the struggle against Israel. They also established a high level of credibility by giving Egypt extensive military and financial aid, an especially effective course at a time when Washington was refusing even token assistance. This marked the beginning of Soviet penetration of the Middle East's Southern Tier through an elaborate network of patron-client relationships in the Arab world. In many respects, the American attempt to check Russian advances in the Middle East by building an alliance system on the Soviet Union's southwestern periphery actually had the opposite effect of opening new areas of influence to the U.S.S.R.

During the following decades the Cold War continued unabated, though its character fluctuated in terms of shifting strategies and the mutual desire to avoid superpower confrontation. The United States and the Soviet Union vied with each other for supremacy in the Middle East, each seeking to enhance its position at the expense of the other. In the mid-1960s, President Johnson, exasperated by Egypt and the "progressive" Arab camp, began to emphasize the American relationship with Israel. This ultimately led to a polarization of the Arab-Israeli conflict in terms of superpower globalism. Though the United States and the Soviet Union cooperated on ending hostilities in the 1967 Arab-Israeli war, they had been forced by their own positions and by the regional situation to take sides in the now escalated dispute. Johnson backed Israel, and the Soviets became committed supporters of the Palestinians and the Arab confrontation states.

Johnson did play a role in inaugurating the new peace process that began with United Nations Security Council Resolution 242 of November 22, 1967, but this also became a facet of the global rivalry. As the peace process changed directions and altered in intensity, Washington and Moscow sought to direct developments in Arab-Israeli relations in ways advantageous to their respective positions in the Middle East. Both powers assigned the success or failure of the process a lower priority than the impact of success or failure on the global power structure in the area. Throughout the 1970s and 1980s, the U.S. and the U.S.S.R. often manipulated the quest for Arab-Israeli peace in their efforts to gain the upper hand in the Middle East political equation.

In the 1970s, the United States constantly shifted its Cold War strategy in the Middle East to outmaneuver the Soviet Union. President Nixon experimented briefly with the peace process, but then concentrated on establishing special surrogates to help limit Soviet activity and influence in the area. President Carter tried to establish a strong American peacemaker image, but never went beyond ending the state of war between Egypt and Israel. He spent the remainder of his term in office securing the Persian Gulf from the threat posed by the Soviet Union and by Iran. At the same time, the Soviets were constantly seeking to shore up and expand their own Middle East surrogate system. Often in a defensive posture with regard to American moves, they had considerable difficulty holding on to their gains of the previous two decades.

Finally, in the 1980s, the global rivalry underwent radical changes. Initially it became more intense, owing to President Reagan's strong anti-Soviet orientation. After the rise to power of

Mikhail Gorbachev, however, the Soviet way of dealing with world politics was largely transformed in keeping with the liberalization at home. This change was instrumental in bringing about a significant shift in the American approach to international issues in general, including those relating to the Middle East.

By the end of his presidency, Reagan had completely altered his original view of the Soviet threat and was actively promoting the new theme of superpower cooperation. In the Middle East, he took more interest in a comprehensive Arab-Israeli peace than at any previous time, and he had begun to make some headway toward a settlement when his second term ended. President Bush picked up where Reagan and Secretary of State George Shultz had left off, seeking to resolve the Arab-Israeli conflict while preserving a cordial relationship with the Soviet Union in the post–Cold War era.

The themes and strategies of the superpower rivalry in the Middle East varied in emphasis and intensity. Both sides sought to establish dominance in the area. Each had its successes and failures; but both, preoccupied as they were with the exigencies of their global competition, had difficulty dealing effectively with the regional dynamics involved. The dilemma they faced lay in determining the proper balance between the global and regional approaches to the formulation of Middle East policy.

Global and Regional Approaches to Middle East Policy

Though the superpowers were always aware of the global and regional factors in the Mideast equation, they generally assigned a higher priority to gaining the advantage in their rivalry with each other than to assisting the needs and aspirations of the indigenous states. The globalization of Middle East policy included a variety of tactical moves on both sides, often comparable in essence though different in style. Access to or control of the area's major ports and waterways was a common objective. Petroleum was another important issue, with the Americans intent on ensuring its continuing availability and the Soviets anxious to end exclusive Western domination of its production and distribution.

The superpowers also attached great importance to establishing cooperative relationships with Middle Eastern states. These included both alliances or "fronts" with groups of countries and bilateral accords designed to provide strategic advantages. In general, such agreements involved manipulation of the regional powers to accommodate the broader geopolitical goals of Washington and Moscow. Often the superpowers' policy requirements diverged from those of their regional allies. The superpowers were mainly concerned with global aims, whereas the local states usually had to take regional politics into serious consideration in order to protect their own viability. On those occasions when Washington or Moscow tried to force their surrogates to conform to their own policies, a conflict of interests often arose.

American global policy toward the Middle East began under the Truman administration after the end of World War II. Soviet attempts to establish footholds in the area in the immediate postwar period alarmed the United States and led to a number of efforts to "contain" the Russian threat. The Truman Doctrine was perhaps the most dramatic move in this direction, and the rest of Truman's Mideast policy was geared to it. The principal objective was to block Soviet incursions, whether territorial or political.

Though the Truman administration was involved in some of the regional developments of the time, notably the emergence of the State of Israel, these changes in the local situation were subordinated to the more important containment policy. Following the Soviet departure from Iranian Azerbaijan and the successful outcome of the Truman Doctrine, the administration concentrated on trying to stabilize the existing status quo in the Middle East. It also tried to draw some of the local powers into a regional defense system.

A 1950 agreement with Great Britain and France guaranteeing established borders in the region was designed to prevent dislocations and preclude any Soviet-inspired alterations in the prevailing political structure. In practice, this agreement was never the basis of concrete policy, except when invoked by Eisenhower in 1956 to resolve the Suez crisis.

The regional defense project concentrated on the idea of making Egypt the key partner in an American-sponsored alliance system. It never made any headway because it ignored Egyptian objections to such a pact, a classic example of a global policy foundering on regional obstructions.

The Eisenhower administration was equally preoccupied with Cold War global concerns. Despite the president's determined move to secure Israel's evacuation of Sinai after the Suez crisis, his principal aim was to hold the line against the Soviets in the Middle East, as well as in other areas. Secretary of State John Foster Dulles was in complete accord with him in this respect. The 1955 Baghdad Pact represented the fruition of Truman's earlier attempts to build a Mideast defense system. The Eisenhower Doctrine, which became the basis of U.S. policy toward the region two years later, was a perfect expression of the "anti-communist" orientation of the United States of that time. Its almost exclusive interest in protecting local countries from Soviet designs, however, made it virtually impossible for the administration to deal effectively with regional political developments, among them the powerful force of Arab nationalism.

During the brief presidency of John F. Kennedy, no concrete Middle East policy was ever developed, partly because concern with other areas diverted attention elsewhere. The succeeding Johnson administration gradually became deeply involved in Middle East affairs, but its ultimate policy, like Truman's and Eisenhower's, reflected a global rather than a regional approach. The continuing struggle against communism in Vietnam undoubtedly played an important role in Johnson's way of dealing with international issues.

A key factor in Johnson's attitude toward the Middle East political equation was his negative reaction to Nasser, whom he regarded as pro-Soviet. By 1966 he had decided on a policy that was at the same time hostile toward Egypt and cooperative with the Israelis. Though he later became quite involved in the peace process, he never really broke the tie to Israel. Indeed, convinced that Israel had become an irreplaceable surrogate of the United States in the Middle East, he became more closely allied with that country than any other president before him. Other regional considerations were not allowed to interfere with the "special relationship" between the two countries, of which he was the principal architect.

The Nixon administration experimented with global and regional approaches to the Middle East, but for the most part global priorities prevailed, thanks in good part to the views of Henry Kissinger, which are discussed in Chapter 3. Kissinger, first as national security advisor and then as secretary of state, dominated Nixon's foreign policy. A committed globalist who admired the traditions of nineteenth-century European diplomacy, he was concerned above all to keep the Soviet Union from making advances at America's expense. To this end he hoped to construct a system of superpower détente that would preserve world peace. In his view, everything else had to be subordinated to his grand design of restricting the Soviet Union to a manageable role in a carefully crafted international order.

What this meant in practice was that all regional concerns and all projects for Middle East conflict resolution came to be seen either as relatively unimportant or as obstructions to the broader project. Though Nixon made periodic efforts to promote peace or reassure the Arabs of his impartiality, Kissinger assigned a low priority to the Mideast peace process and emphasized the importance of Israel as a partner in the American attempt to limit Soviet influence in the area. In the end, his preferences predominated.

Jimmy Carter, by contrast, took a genuine interest in regional needs and aspirations, and in revitalizing the peace process. Ultimately, however, he was forced to settle for something less than the comprehensive peace he wanted, and had to turn to a more globally oriented policy because of the Soviet invasion of Afghanistan and the threat posed by the overthrow of the shah and the rise to power in Iran of the avowedly anti-American Ayatollah Khomeini. The 1980 Carter Doctrine was focused on the Persian Gulf; it proclaimed a protective U.S. attitude toward this strategic region in extremely forceful terms. Though Carter would have liked to moderate Washington's traditional globalism in favor of a regional approach to the Middle East, he was in the final analysis compelled by circumstances beyond his control to revert to an essentially global orientation.

President Reagan never really understood or cared much about the regional dynamics of the Middle East. He was forced by the repercussions of the Israeli invasion of Lebanon in 1982 to make some gestures in the direction of conflict resolution, but they achieved nothing. Instead, the drift of U.S. Middle East policy was toward reliance on surrogates, especially Israel and the shaky government in Lebanon, to uphold American interests in the area. Regional problems and the tenuous road to peace were all but lost in this context.

By the time George Bush assumed the presidency, dramatic changes had taken place in international politics, notably the emergence of a relatively moderate regime in Moscow under the direction of Mikhail Gorbachev. Then, during Bush's first year in the White House, powerful liberalizing movements broke out in eastern Europe and other regions. In the context of increasing cooperation between the superpowers, both leaders put aside the earlier Soviet-American rivalry and began addressing regional conflicts and dislocations, most prominently the Gulf crisis of 1990–91. However, though Bush and Gorbachev are far freer than their predecessors to develop a regional approach to the Middle East, they will ultimately have to deal with more than attempts to alter the status quo by military force. They also need to find ways to resolve the Arab-Israeli conflict and to promote more equitable and democratic traditions throughout the region to provide a foundation for long-term political stability.

The Soviet Union also assigned priority to global considerations in its postwar Middle East policy. In the initial Stalinist period, there was almost no deference to regional concerns. The emphasis was on territorial intrusion and communist subversion, with little regard for the nationalist aspirations of the indigenous peoples. During the Khrushchev era there was a gradual shift toward support for Middle East nationalism, with the Soviets expressing sympathy with its aims and offering economic and military aid to achieve specific goals. This endorsement of a degree of regionalism in the Soviet approach enhanced Moscow's standing in the area enormously. By supporting popular indigenous movements, the Soviets increased their regional appeal and facilitated the construction of an extensive system of patron-client relationships. Because of the degree to which this approach had boosted the Soviet image, Leonid Brezhnev continued to make it the basis of his Mideast policy from 1964 to 1982.

The Soviet appeal to regional forces was stereotyped and often concealed a thinly veiled form of globalism in which the underlying and often obsessive aim was to displace or outmaneuver the United States in the Middle East. Though an extremely large amount of Soviet military and economic aid was given to Egypt and other Arab states, and cooperative agreements were reached with Turkey and Iran, the Soviets did little to help resolve the more profound sociopolitical problems of the region. Yet the very fact of articulating sympathy and concern and actually giving material help had its rewards. Certainly, it made the Soviet competitive position considerably more viable.

In the case of Afghanistan, which is examined in detail in Chapter 4, Moscow allowed a local political shift that seemed to offer advantages for the Soviet Union's strategic position throughout the area to obscure the prevailing sentiments of the

Afghan people. The result was catastrophic; it took the perceptive genius and courage of Gorbachev to extricate the U.S.S.R. from the dangerous quagmire of Afghanistan. Gorbachev also developed a far more perceptive regional approach to the area, as mentioned earlier.

During the decades when the Soviet-American rivalry was intense, both superpowers necessarily dealt with the Middle East from a global perspective. The stakes were so high that the superpower struggle had to be given priority. But this did not alter the fact that powerful regional sociopolitical forces were part of the equation. The failure of the United States and the Soviet Union to take the regional factor into sufficient account has been costly for both sides.

The concentration on achieving tactical advantages in the global power game caused them seriously to miscalculate the urgency of local issues and problems, and the impact that disregarding them could have on superpower relations with the indigenous states. Periodically, there were attempts to deal effectively with the elusive question of regional political dynamics. However, these were often not adequately sustained or developed into comprehensive and consistent policies. Yet the regional problem always remained a potent force with which the superpowers had to contend, whether they realized it or not.

The regional dimension is often referred to by Middle East specialists as "the situation on the ground." What is meant by this is the political climate and the complex interaction of social forces within particular countries or blocs and throughout the region as a whole. The most important underlying reality about the Middle East is that the societies within it are in a process of transition from a traditional to a "modern" cultural orientation that is predominantly Western and secular. The impact on the Middle Eastern psyche of the intrusion of the West in the nineteenth and twentieth centuries, the quest for reform, and the subsequent experimentation with Western institutions and lifestyles have been profound and unsettling. The dislocations, abuses, and inequities attending this transition have aroused fear, uncertainty, and raw anger. Individuals, groups, and large masses of the population have been driven to the brink of desperation and hysteria, and violence has been common.

The most sensitive issues in this volatile demographic landscape have been malpractice in domestic politics, regional conflicts, and the remnants of imperialism and other forms of foreign intervention. The change from traditional Islamic polities, such as the Ottoman Empire, to the secular nationalist order that took over in much of the Middle East after World War I brought new political elites to power. Some became involved in various forms of corruption and compromise, and were replaced by revisionist elites. Ultimately, many segments of the population became disenchanted with the reformist governments as well, leaving a residue of bitter feelings toward the established order.

One of the main grievances in recent decades has been the monopolization of political and economic power by the shah in Iran and by some of the self-styled "progressive" regimes in the Arab world. In the countries in which opposition parties were not tolerated, the only available vehicle of dissent from the status quo was Islamic resurgence. This thrust a number of relatively new neofundamentalist organizations into the mainstream of Middle East politics.

A dominant characteristic of the neofundamentalist groups has been their pronounced populism. Unlike the nineteenth-century Islamic reform movements, they sought to galvanize vast segments of the disaffected populace into action against the established order. When their message of vehement and uncompromising opposition to the status quo took root in the soil of mass alienation, a powerful political force was unleashed, one that neither the ruling elites nor the superpowers could comprehend or control. In 1978–79, the rage of angry Iranians, carefully orchestrated by Ayatollah Khomeini, toppled the shah's regime in a massive uprising.

Starting in 1979 and throughout the early 1980s, Islamic militants engaged in bloody encounters with Asad's troops and security forces in northern Syria. Though the regime ultimately prevailed, neofundamentalists representing much larger segments of the population had demonstrated their ability to challenge the rulers of an authoritarian one-party state. The tension generated by this challenge has never really disappeared, and Asad remains somewhat off balance thanks to a latent opposition that rejects his legitimacy.

On October 6, 1981, the eighth anniversary of the surprise Egyptian attack on Israel's Bar Lev Line, members of the radical Islamic Jihad Organization assassinated Egypt's President Sadat while he was reviewing a parade to honor the occasion. No revolution followed, and Sadat's successor, Husni Mubarak, kept the country on an even course through his more moderate political style. Yet the neofundamentalist Islamic movement, which had been increasingly significant since the 1967 war, continues to operate as an only partly visible counterculture, a form of opposition and a potential source of future destabilization.

It is clear from all these occurrences that politics has gone to the "street" in much of the Middle East, and this is the single most important fact about the "situation on the ground" in the past twenty years. Movements arising among the grass roots and demanding radical change have become part of the political equation. The Iranian case, which astonished most policymakers and Middle East specialists, should serve as a dramatic warning that the potential power of mass action can no longer be ignored, especially when it is harnessed by determined leaders who can read the public mood and make it a vehicle of revolution and transition.

The relevance of this phenomenon for the political elites in Washington and Moscow was dramatically illustrated by developments in Iran and Afghanistan in the late 1970s and late 1980s, respectively. The United States had for decades considered the shah of Iran a principal surrogate in the American security system. His relationship to his own people was considered unimportant and was ignored in the process of defining the Iranian connection in U.S. policy. The deterioration of the political situation in the country, never clearly seen in Washington, was the result of a growing rupture between the shah and large segments of the population, which considered his regime increasingly repressive. Yet from the American perspective, all that mattered in the long run was the shah's role in the global picture. When the regime suddenly fell from power, the Carter administration, albeit one particularly sensitive to the regional dimension, was forced to rethink U.S. policy toward Iran. Even a decade later, there is considerable uncertainty about what shape it should take.

Soviet policy in Afghanistan also ran into difficulty because the Kremlin misread the regional situation. In its eagerness to capitalize on the unexpected rise to power of Afghan communists, the Soviet leadership completely overlooked the relationship between the Afghan people and the new government. As the popular alienation from the regime developed into a massive uprising and civil war, Moscow intervened to bring the centrifugal forces under control. Later forced to shift its ground, it ultimately had to withdraw entirely from the ill-fated venture. Like the United States in Iran, the Soviets were badly hurt by their own miscalculations in Afghanistan, and they have yet to devise a viable policy toward this volatile neighbor.

Regional conflicts are another major source of grievance in the Middle East. There are a number of rivalries and local confrontations in the area, but the Arab-Israeli dispute is by far the largest and the most unsettling. The problem has been both aggravated and ameliorated by the immediate parties and external actors. But its prolongation is costly in human terms for those directly involved, though the superpowers have tended to deal with it in terms of tactical maneuvering in their own rivalry.

The United States has taken serious interest in the Arab-Israeli peace process since the 1967 war. Yet it has often put global considerations ahead of conflict resolution, frequently leading to delays and sometimes to obstruction of the quest for compromise and negotiation. What is left out of consideration when this happens is the explosive impact allowing the peace process to founder has on Palestinians and their supporters in the Arab world.

Those in charge of U.S. Middle East policy need to remember that the establishment of Israel entailed the destruction of Palestine and the uprooting and dispersion of hundreds of thousands of Palestinians. It was a form of patricide, and as such was a profoundly traumatic experience for its victims. This transformation of Palestine created an abiding bitterness among the Palestinians and their friends, a grievance that escalated rather than diminished with the passage of time.

Much of the terrorism connected with the Palestinian problem arose from this grievance, and no matter how repugnant it may have been to the outside world as well as counterproductive to the Palestinian cause, it has nevertheless been responsible for adverse developments and disturbing dislocations in the regional system. Also, attempts to contain it have on occasion led to ill-considered retaliatory actions by the United States that were harmful to American interests in the long run.

The most important recent manifestation of the latent political power embodied in the residue of Palestinian alienation is the *intifada* that began in December 1987. The Israeli occupation of the West Bank and Gaza had always involved a degree of tension and incidental confrontations. But the *intifada* represented a rejection of Israeli rule on a larger scale than ever before. Young Palestinians began throwing stones at the authorities on a regular basis until it became a continuing uprising that the Israelis have never been able to contain successfully. The *intifada* established a new dimension of the Arab-Israeli conflict, one that seems likely to have a lasting impact on the peace process and the tactical positions of each side. It is also another example of the movement of Middle East politics to the street, and in this respect it could have even broader repercussions.

The Soviet Union has been generally supportive of the Palestinians and the Arab side in the conflict, giving massive military aid to some of the Arab confrontation states on occasion. Yet Moscow's primary aim appears to have been to establish a major role for itself in the peace process. This has reflected a greater interest in gaining an advantageous position in the global rivalry than in assigning the highest priority to resolution of the conflict. The regional approach of the Soviets has therefore been qualified by its relationship to the global balance of power.

The remnants of imperialism and other forms of foreign intervention have been another source of discontent in the fluid and volatile political landscape of the Middle East. Neo-imperialism, the contemporary extension of nineteenth-century colonialism in the area, is perceived by the indigenous peoples as the political manipulation of forces and events by the superpowers in particular. The most evident manifestations of neo-imperialism have been the attempts of Washington and Moscow to recruit surrogates to assist them in consolidating their respective security systems in the Middle East.

The formation of the Baghdad Pact in 1955 was deeply disturbing to the states that did not adhere to it. They saw it as an alliance between the U.S. and the U.K. and the ruling elites of the Middle Eastern signatory powers. It represented the interests of Western neo-imperialism and self-serving regimes, not the well-being of the people in the countries involved.

The regional states that subsequently entered into patron-client relationships with Washington, referred to as surrogates or partners by the Nixon Doctrine, were also seen as collaborators throughout much of the area. Israel and Iran in particular were widely regarded as agents of U.S. policy and enemies of the public good in the Middle East. Israel, which was even more insensitive to the regional mood than the United States, was widely regarded in the Arab world as being deeply involved in a virtual conspiracy with Washington directed against the Arabs in general and the Palestinians in particular. For many, the shah had the same kind of relationship with Washington. As a despot, concerned only with his own wealth and power, he was willing to ally himself with the U.S. to advance his own interests at the expense of his people, and willing to supply Israel with oil in exchange for assistance in maintaining his repressive regime, as well as to oblige the Americans.

The United States also recruited less important surrogates to further its global aims. A good example is the relationship between the Reagan administration and President Amin Gemayel of Lebanon, examined in detail in Chapter 3. When the situation in Lebanon became highly destabilized a few months after the Israeli invasion in June 1982, Washington formed a tacit alliance with Israel and President Gemayel designed to establish a political dispensation favorable to the interests of all partners. This ran directly counter to the aspirations of the majority opposition groups in the country, and following several military encounters that had devastating results for the U.S., Israel, and Gemayel, the alliance and all the plans connected with it had to be cancelled. It was yet another example of regional forces prevailing over a misconceived tactical operation keyed to U.S. global objectives.

Other regional friends of the United States included Saudi Arabia, Morocco, Oman, Turkey, and, to a lesser extent, Jordan. Because forming some sort of cooperative relationship with the United States has been perceived as advantageous to these countries for various reasons, they became active partners in one way or another. Their major problem with the arrangements they concluded with Washington was the fact that often they could not conform to American policy without damaging their viability in the eyes of their neighbors and their own people. Saudi Arabia, which has a somewhat tenuous position in the context of inter-Arab politics, has to place limits on the degree to which it can accommodate American policy. Should it go too far in this direction, it could seriously damage its own regional viability and even threaten the regime itself.

The Soviets had similar problems with their surrogates.

Though they spent large sums of money supplying countries like Egypt and devoted a great deal of time and energy in trying to form an "anti-imperialist" front among the Arabs, their clients either refused to shape their foreign policies in accordance with Moscow's or abandoned the Soviet sphere altogether. The general unreliability of the states Moscow tried to enlist in its security system was highly frustrating for the architects of Soviet Middle East policy, and eventually the whole program was greatly diminished by Gorbachev.

The regional aspects of the Middle Eastern political equation have become increasingly important for the superpowers since the Iraqi invasion of Kuwait in August 1990 and the crisis and war that followed. It is no longer possible for the superpowers to ignore regional political considerations in the Middle East. With the movement of politics to the street, there is little tolerance left in Middle Eastern societies for foreign exploitation or even for special arrangements between particular power elites and the superpowers. It has been definitively shown that regional forces, no matter how much weaker than the superpowers they may be in a purely military sense, have a formidable ability to disrupt or outmaneuver the global designs of the Americans and the Soviets.

Like Gulliver in Lilliput, the superpowers are far more powerful than the today's Middle Eastern states and like him they find it difficult to read the local situation with much accuracy. In the end, Gulliver found himself in an untenable situation, forcing him to flee to the neighboring kingdom of miniature people and eventually to leave the region entirely. The superpowers have also had to terminate many of their alliances and bilateral agreements with Middle Eastern states and to back out of situations in order to minimize their losses. For though the regional states are relatively weak, the sociopolitical forces that are active within them are very powerful and difficult to manage. Indeed, they are capable of undermining the tactical moves of Washington and Moscow, and have effectively done so on several occasions. For this reason, Washington and Moscow have assigned higher pri-

ority to regional considerations. Whether they have done so to an
adequate extent remains to be seen.

Decision-Making and Its Consequences

The superpowers, and all states for that matter, are free to
adopt whatever policies they think will advance the national
interests they have designated, though they have to accept the
consequences of the policies they adopt. An important reality
about superpower decision-making is that it has to operate in
terms of specific constraints. In the American case, these constraints arise from the political system and the functional structure of the executive foreign policy establishment.

As William Quandt, the Middle East specialist on President
Carter's National Security Council, has pointed out, "Domestic
political considerations must always be taken into account if a
president wishes to use his influence effectively."[3] The forces in
American politics that restrict a president's freedom of action
include Congressional action, the pressure exercised by lobbies,
and public opinion. In formulating Middle East policy, the chief
executive has to contend with the powerful Israeli lobby, run
principally by the American Israel Public Affairs Committee
(AIPAC), and with Congress, which is strongly influenced by
AIPAC and by the political power of American Jews.[4]

The pressure brought to bear on U.S. Middle East policymaking by the combined influence of Congress and AIPAC is enormous. Seth Tillman, who was able to observe this pressure at
close range as Senator Fulbright's assistant, has summarized the
effect of this phenomenon succinctly:

> Since the creation of Israel, and increasingly with the
> development of the powerful Israeli lobby in the United

3. William B. Quandt, *Camp David: Peacemaking and Politics* (Washington, D.C.: Brookings Institution, 1986), p. 6.
4. See Paul Findley, *They Dare to Speak Out: People and Institutions
Confront Israel's Lobby* (Westport, CT: Lawrence Hill, 1985); Edward Tivnan, *The Lobby: Jewish Political Power and American Foreign Policy* (New
York: Simon & Schuster, 1987).

States in the sixties and seventies, virtually every American effort to defend and advance American interests in the Middle East—interests ranging from peace to détente to energy—has been immediately converted from a foreign to a domestic problem. That fact has been the principal obstacle to the formulation of an American policy based on the totality of American interests in a vital and dangerous region.[5]

Because of AIPAC's power over a Congress that can restrict a president's options in making international political decisions through its control of the budget, Middle East policy is usually made at the presidential level.[6] This has on occasion distanced the president's closest advisors from the foreign policy and national security bureaucracies, leaving the former free to formulate policy in terms of domestic politics or in accordance with particular theories of international relations, while diminishing or circumventing the advisory role of the latter.

The way this has worked out in practice is that successive administrations have avoided taking any action that might be interpreted as hostile to Israel, both to preserve the support of American Jewry and to maintain Israel as an "indispensable" surrogate. At the same time, the usually strong preference of high-level advisors for the global approach to international issues has generally limited the efforts of the foreign policy bureaucracy to get the president to deal with the Middle East in terms of "on the ground" realities.

With reference to he handling of the 1970 crisis in Jordan, Alan Dowty explains:

Middle East experts in the Departments of State and Defense were very critical of this [top-level global] approach. Though framing the crisis as a U.S.-Soviet confrontation

5. Seth P. Tillman, *The United States in the Middle East: Interests and Obstacles* (Bloomington, IN: Indiana University Press, 1982), pp. 288–89.
6. Quandt, p. 8.

might suit White House political needs, they suggested, it overrated the Soviets' conrol of their clients and their interest in Jordan, while overlooking important U.S. interests in the Middle East that were independent of Soviet relations. This lack of appreciation of local dimensions led, it was said, to a situation in which Nixon and Kissinger could be manipulated by local parties (Israel and Hussein). In short, facing down Moscow might be useful in the short run, but left behind a policy ill-suited to regional trends and to the maintenance of healthy U.S.-Arab relations. These experts would argue later that this global fixation had contributed to the conditions out of which the 1973 war developed.[7]

Globalism, pressure from the Israeli lobby, and the consequent minimization of the foreign policy bureaucracy's role in decision-making have made it difficult for American presidents to construct a U.S. Middle East policy designed to serve U.S. interests by dealing effectively with the sociopolitical dynamics of the region. The quest for peace has been hampered, American credibility has been seriously undermined, and disruptive forces have been engendered by the reactions to many of the dislocations that have resulted in part from the shortcomings of Washington's official approach to the area.

A number of presidents have at least tried to overcome the disabilities of this circumstantial barrier to a more enlightened Middle East policy. Eisenhower took a bold position in opposition to Israel's occupation of Sinai in 1956, and ultimately forced it to withdraw. Yet later he was drawn back into the global perspective that had dominated the earlier work of Dulles in forming the Baghdad Pact. The Eisenhower Doctrine of 1957 had virtually no reference to regional forces and no strategy for handling them effectively.

Johnson made what could have been a constructive step in the

7. Alan Dowty, *Middle East Crisis: U.S. Decision-Making in 1958, 1970, and 1973* (Berkeley and Los Angeles: University of California Press, 1984), p. 151.

direction of a comprehensive resolution of the Arab-Israeli conflict, but in the end held on to the tacit alliance he had formed with Israel and allowed the opportunity for peace to slip through his hands. He was so preoccupied with the global issue of containing the Soviets in Vietnam, the Middle East, and elsewhere that he could never orchestrate a regional approach to the complex problems of the Middle East. His sensitivity to the controversial nature of Mideast policy in American politics also undoubtedly played a role in his decision not to break new ground.

Nixon seriously intended to revise Middle East policy in a way that would take the regional factors into consideration. He experimented with the peace process during his first year in office and tried to reassure the Arabs of his impartiality near the end of his abbreviated presidency. For the most part, however, he was strongly influenced by Kissinger's pronounced globalism and allowed the regional initiatives to lapse into oblivion.

Ford tried to adopt a tougher way of handling Israel, but this never became part of a more broadly defined and implemented Middle East policy. His successor, Jimmy Carter, starting where Ford had left off, sought to construct an innovative and imaginative Middle East policy oriented in terms of the peace process. But the intransigence of Israeli Prime Minister Menachem Begin and American Jewish pressure on the White House, combined with Carter's own feeling that he had to accomplish at least something in the Middle East, ultimately forced him to settle for an Egyptian-Israeli peace, which in many respects circumvented the crucial underlying problems and fell short of his original goal.

Reagan was so obsessed with the global struggle against the Soviet Union that he paid little attention to regional questions. Despite a brief and insubstantial attempt to reactivate the peace process, he tightened the tacit alliance with Israel and made little real contribution to a comprehensive resolution of the Arab-Israeli conflict.

George Bush, however, was more perspicacious on foreign

policy issues, and also had the good fortune to be president at a time when the Cold War was coming to an end. Given his command of international affairs and the improved climate of world politics, it was certainly to be expected that he would make some progress on the peace process and other problems confronting the Middle East. Addressing the 1990 Gulf crisis, he worked with Gorbachev to establish a joint superpower opposition to the use of military force as an instrument of territorial change in the Middle East, though he had difficulty earlier in handling the Arab-Israeli peace process.

Whatever the extenuating circumstances may be, policy is what the president and his advisors make it. And what it is determines whether it will serve American interests or be counterproductive to them. The United States does have real and important interests in the Middle East. Heretofore American policy toward the area has to a considerable extent failed to accomplish what was needed to serve properly the nation's interests. There are, however, a number of factors in the present situation that open new options and new opportunities. With the right choices, therefore, it is possible for unprecedented progress to be made in the 1990s.

Soviet decision-making has been encumbered with similar problems. These derived not so much from the political system, which has left those in charge of Middle East policy relatively free to do what they wanted, as from the rigid and stylized way in which the Soviet ruling elite looked at the world and related to Third World countries, despite the fact that policy is often made in consultation with academic and other area specialists. Perhaps even more obsessed with the global rivalry than U.S. presidents and their advisors, Kremlin leaders before Gorbachev adopted an inflexible view of U.S. "imperialism" as a menace to all progressive forces in the world. It therefore had to be combatted whenever and wherever possible. The only qualifying exception was that some form of détente had to be maintained to prevent a superpower confrontation.

This left little room for compromise or cooperative ventures with the United States. It also helped to keep Soviet relations with Iran and Turkey on a limited economic level and to narrow those with the Arab world to an "anti-imperialist" front kind of relationship. As a result of the policy orientation of Khrushchev and of Brezhnev and Kosygin, combined with the disastrous intervention in Afghanistan, the Soviet position in the Middle East was extremely tenuous by the mid-1980s.

Gorbachev, however, was a very different kind of leader. He had the wisdom and courage to see what was wrong with Soviet Middle East policy and to change it rapidly and drastically. By pulling out of Afghanistan, moving away from the "anti-imperialist" tactic in favor of pragmatic relationships with all Middle Eastern countries, and promoting Soviet-American cordiality, he transformed Moscow's standing and stature in the Middle East and the world. If he and his successors can bring the Soviet Union into the peace process, they will have achieved the kind of viability and influence in the area that their predecessors were unable to effect with their less imaginative and largely global approach to the Middle East.

The attempts of both superpowers to shape an effective Middle East policy have been frustrating and unrewarding, owing not so much to external obstacles as to their inability to approach the area in terms of its own sociopolitical dynamics. Globalism has been the major stumbling block because it has prevented them from seeing that the indigenous forces are more important than they ever imagined. The untoward consequences of the formulation of Middle East policy in the context of global theory have been considerable. The challenge confronting decision-makers in Washington and Moscow in the radically changed world of the 1990s is, therefore, to find a way of incorporating a realistic regional dimension in their approach to a complicated area. They appear to have already begun to do this in a determined way.

3   AMERICAN POLICY

ONTEMPORARY American Middle East policy stems from the need to define and protect the interests of the United States in an area where Washington had played virtually no political role prior to World War II. The circumstances surrounding the new international structure that came into being in 1945 forced the United States to play an unusually active role in this region. This was because its Western allies were unable to maintain their former positions of strength there at the very time the Soviet Union was trying to expand its influence into the Northern Tier. With little experience and only a vague pro-American attitude among the indigenous peoples in their favor, U.S. decision-makers addressed themselves to the task of outlining their strategic goals and tactical doctrines to meet the Soviet challenge and establish a viable American presence in the Middle East.

Strategic Goals and Tactical Doctrines

The overriding concern of American foreign policy in the immediate postwar period was finding an effective way to check Soviet expansionism throughout the world. When applied to the Middle East, this meant using all means available to prevent the Russians from filling the power vacuum being created by the incipient withdrawal of the old colonial powers. The undisguised Soviet attempts to establish footholds in an area where Western influence was receding intensified American apprehensions and made containment Washington's highest priority in the Middle East. This necessarily involved a competitive situation in which the United States was actively seeking to establish its own positions of strength while blocking Soviet advances into the same area.

A closely related interest was maintaining access to the facilities and resources of the Middle East. Great Britain and France had traditionally enjoyed special status with regard to the region's ports and waterways, at least to the extent of preventing the Russians from controlling them. This gave them a decided advantage in the great power diplomatic game of the nineteenth century.

The Turkish Straits, the Suez Canal and other Red Sea passageways, and the Persian Gulf, as well as the important ports located in these areas, are strategically vital in any rivalry for a dominant position in this international crossroads that links Europe, Asia, and Africa. Policy-makers in Washington were determined to secure access to or control over these facilities in the light of the Soviet Union's aggressive moves in the Middle East after the war.

The region was also valued for its vast petroleum reserves. This became an increasingly important aspect of the superpower rivalry in the succeeding decades, particularly because of the dependence of America's European allies on Middle East oil. In time, the flow of this key resource to the West came to be considered essential. Any attempt by the Soviet Union or the regional states to interfere with it, therefore, could not be tolerated.

The interrelated objectives of containing Soviet attempts to gain the upper hand in the Middle East and preserving access to the region's strategic facilities and vital resources required the development of effective tactical doctrines to attain the designated goals. The focus of U.S. Middle East policy-making was on developing and refining these doctrines. Reduced to absolute basics, they included the promotion of peace and stability and the recruitment of regional partners to assist the United States in containing the Soviet Union.

Promoting peace and stability was initially interpreted as

guaranteeing the territorial status quo and keeping the established political order in place as much as possible. It was believed that the prevention of radical change would keep the Russians at bay and facilitate American ascendancy in the area. Later this tactic evolved into a particular interest in resolving the Arab-Israeli conflict, regarded by many as a major source of regional destabilization. The "peace process," as it came to be called, emerged as the principal activity related to this aspect of American Middle East policy.

The doctrine of recruiting regional partners also grew out of the attempt to preserve the territorial and political status quo, but quickly diverged into another kind of activity. At first it moved in the direction of setting up an alliance system, but later it evolved into a quest for surrogates on different levels. The principal theme in this case was to bring as many of the regional states as possible into a cooperative venture designed to minimize the influence and leverage of the Soviet Union in the Middle East.

The formulation of American Middle East policy has been based on the interaction of these two tactical doctrines. Though they may have emerged from a common source—the commitment to uphold the status quo—they ultimately diverged and even came into conflict with each other. The underlying tension between the two endeavors stems from their relationship to the global and regional approaches discussed in Chapter 2. The peace process has a regional orientation in that it is aimed at resolving a conflict that has entailed major dislocations in the regional system. Yet it is also connected to the global approach inasmuch as the way it has been handled by Washington has to a considerable extent been determined by the exigencies of the rivalry with the Soviet Union.

A subtle distinction has to be made about the relationship between the Soviet challenge and American attitudes toward Middle East peace. On some occasions, U.S. decision-makers have been unable to deal effectively with regional issues, including the peace process, when the Soviet threat was not salient. For example, the fact that Moscow had not made the PLO an integral part of its regional security system made it seem less urgent in Washington that the Palestinian question be addressed and resolved. This left successive administrations, from Johnson to Reagan, free to pursue partial or limited peace initiatives that did not include the more fundamental and more difficult issue of Palestinian self-determination.

On the other hand, the existence of the Soviet-American rivalry encouraged Washington's reliance on Israel as its principal surrogate. In this respect, the global concern about Russian influence in the Middle East inclined American policy-makers to emphasize their support for Israel and assign a lower priority to the peace process, which Israel usually wanted to avoid or delay. That is to say, the absence of a Soviet connection induced an American retreat from the peace objective in some instances, and the presence of a Soviet connection had the same effect in other cases. This raises the question of exactly what conditions would incline U.S. decision-makers to develop a determined and regionally oriented peace policy. It may be that the removal of an overriding preoccupation with the Soviet threat to American interests, eliminating the need to have a salient global factor or a principal surrogate, will produce the requisite conditions for such a change in Washington's approach to peace.

In the past, however, the quest for surrogates has been almost exclusively a global undertaking: that is, the choice of particular states as partners has been specifically designed to restrict Soviet power and influence in the Middle East. Since the Jewish state became the most important local ally of the United States in the area, what came to be known as Washington's "special relationship" with Israel is actually the dissonant link between the peace process as a regional policy and the recruitment of surrogates on the basis of global deterrence.

On the one hand, Israel is an immediate party to the Arab-Israeli dispute—one of the two sides in the conflict and a principal negotiator in all discussions designed to lead to peace.

Thus, as seen from the American position as mediator, it is an entity to be influenced or persuaded or pressured into cooperating with initiatives either launched by or approved by the United States. The American approach to Israel in this respect is nonpartisan and pragmatic.

On the other hand, Israel as an "indispensable" surrogate is a regional power with theoretically parallel interests to those of the United States. It is therefore to be accommodated, armed, assisted economically, trusted, and included in Washington's diplomatic and military planning for the Middle East. When this view prevails, Israel's interests and foreign policy requisites are given priority, even if this is counterproductive to the peace process, which is often the case. Hence, the peace and surrogate tactics collided in the context of America's Israeli connection, confronting successive administrations with the dilemma of having to choose between stabilizing the area through conflict resolution and maintaining what was considered the key partner in the U.S.-sponsored regional defense system.

The perplexing relationship between peacemaking as part of a regional orientation and partner recruitment as a major dimension of the global approach lies at the heart of Washington's difficulties in establishing and implementing a Middle East policy geared to its long-range interests. The ways in which different administrations have understood and tried to implement these tactical approaches to containing the Soviets and preserving access to the region's facilities and resources need to be examined and analyzed to understand the motivations and the repercussions of each shift in policy. If the United States is to develop a more rewarding Middle East policy, the mistakes of the past and the reasons for them must be taken into account before the guidelines of a different approach can be determined.

Initial Efforts to Preserve Peace and Stability

The first American attempt to promote peace in the Middle East regional context was President Truman's belated and ineffectual effort to avoid the outbreak of war in Palestine in early

1948. The suggestion by his administration that a United Nations trusteeship be established instead of trying to implement partition, which will come under discussion later, was designed to prevent open hostilities between the emerging Jewish state and the Palestinians and the surrounding Arab countries. Under domestic and foreign pressure, Truman withdrew the proposal and the two sides drifted toward war.

After the 1948 confrontation, the administration was unable to produce any plan for managing the uneasy truce that prevailed in the Arab-Israeli conflict. In 1950, however, it decided to assume the role of guarantor of the status quo in the Middle East as a way of promoting a degree of stability that would act as a deterrent to regional warfare. The United States joined Great Britain and France in issuing the Tripartite Declaration of May 25, 1950. This statement of policy sought to keep the military capabilities of Israel and the Arab states at reasonable levels, to promote peace and stability generally, and to prevent changes in the established boundaries by military force.[1]

The Tripartite Declaration was an extremely rudimentary and relatively ineffective way of keeping the peace and promoting a climate of stability in the Middle East. However, President Eisenhower, who assumed office in January 1953, took it seriously and was actually the only important world leader to enforce it.

Great Britain and France, in blatant contravention of the Declaration, entered into a secret agreement with Israel to attack Egypt and unseat Gamal Abdul Nasser. Tensions rose following an Israeli raid on an Egyptian garrison in Gaza on February 28, 1955, and the situation came to a climax in the summer of 1956, when Nasser nationalized the Suez Canal. An Anglo-French-Israeli attack on Egypt was launched the following October, and met with the immediate condemnation of President Eisenhower.

1. See text in J. C. Hurewitz, *Diplomacy in the Near and Middle East: A Documentary Record*, 2 vols. (Princeton, NJ: Van Nostrand, 1956), 2: 308–9.

This episode will be covered in greater detail later, but it should be noted here that the president's position and subsequent actions, which ultimately led to the complete withdrawal of Israeli forces from Sinai and Gaza, represented a steadfast adherence to the Tripartite Declaration as the proper means of maintaining peace and stability in the Middle East. In a speech on February 20, 1957, Eisenhower articulated what he considered the important principle involved: "If we agree that armed attack can properly achieve the purposes of the assailant, then I fear we will have turned back the clock of international order. We will, in effect, have countenanced the use of force as a means of settling international differences and through this gaining national advantages."[2]

Reaffirmation of the principle of territorial integrity, especially when done in isolation and without subsequent supporting statements, is not enough to have a lasting impact on the peace and stability of a volatile region. Eisenhower's stand, despite its dramatic effect at the time, did little to change the constant escalation of the Arab-Israeli conflict. The president's intentions were certainly constructive and honorable, but his action cannot be considered a peace initiative.

The other aspect of the 1957 settlement was also a temporary stopgap. Stationing a United Nations Emergency Force (UNEF) along the Egyptian-Israeli border and down the east coast of Sinai to Sharm al-Sheikh to prevent a blockade of the Strait of Tiran was a superficial way of dealing with a dispute involving so many complicated ramifications. Though it pacified the conflict for years, it did not address any of the underlying issues. In this respect, it contributed to another outbreak of fighting in 1967.

President Kennedy, who succeeded Eisenhower in January 1961, was anxious to create an American image that reflected sympathy for the aspirations and problems of Third World

2. John Norton Moore, ed., *The Arab-Israeli Conflict: Readings and Documents* (Princeton, NJ: Princeton University Press, 1977), p. 1017.

peoples and governments. The Peace Corps was one manifestation of this policy. In the Middle East, Kennedy tried to repair
U.S.-Arab relations by making overtures to Nasser, reaffirming
continuing support for Saudia Arabia and Jordan, and dealing
with Israel in a broader context of building good relations with a
wide range of Middle East states.[3]

In appointing John Badeau, former president of the American
University in Cairo, as U.S. ambassador to Egypt, Kennedy sig-
nalled his intention to get closer to the "progressive" Arab nationalist countries. Depite some friction with Nasser over his
hostility to Saudi Arabia and Jordan in connection with the
Yemen civil war, the president did conduct an unofficial dialogue
with the Egyptian leader, carried on through special envoys and
Ambassador Badeau.[4]

Though these moves did not lead to a significant improvement
in U.S. relations with Egypt and other Arab nationalist countries, they did result in Kennedy's commitment to the maintenance of peace and stability in the Middle East by reaffirming
American opposition to the use of force as a means of changing
the territorial status quo.[5] This commitment upheld the Tripartite Declaration of 1950 and the principles invoked by Eisenhower after the Suez crisis. But it did not initiate an actual peace
process.

President Johnson initially perpetuated Kennedy's loosely-
defined Middle East policy, seeking to maintain as good a relationship as possible with the conservative and progressive Arab
states while continuing to assist Israel. He also reiterated U.S.
support "for the territorial integrity and political independence
of all countries in the Near East," and opposition "to aggression
and the use of force or threat of force against any country."[6] In

3. Wilbur Crane Eveland, *Ropes of Sand: America's Failure in the Middle East* (New York: Norton, 1980), p. 321.

4. Miles Copeland, *The Game of Nations: The Amorality of Power Politics* (New York: College Notes & Texts, Inc., 1969), pp. 260–67.

5. Department of State, *American Foreign Policy: Current Documents, 1963* (Washington, D.C.: U.S. Government Printing Office, 1967), p. 581.

6. Harry N. Howard, "The United States and the Middle East," in *The*

1966, however, Johnson abandoned this approach to the Middle East in favor of developing a closer working relationship with Israel.

Initial Attempts at Containment

The policy of containing Soviet advances in the world developed gradually during the early postwar years. Its first manifestations in the Middle East were the strong backing given Iran in the 1946 Azerbaijan crisis and the adoption of the Truman Doctrine in 1947. Though neither of these moves suggested the formation of alliances, they marked the beginning of protective relationships with Middle East countries designed to block Soviet intrusiveness.

The Russian attempt to set up puppet regimes in Iranian Azerbaijan and Kurdistan after the agreed date for the evacuation of Allied forces prompted a strong American response that ultimately resulted in the withdrawal of Soviet troops. Moscow also pressured Turkey to revise the Montreux Convention and bring the Straits under the control of the Black Sea powers, a change staunchly resisted by the Ankara government. A similar demand was placed on Greece to provide a naval base in the Dodecanese Islands, a request that was not well received because of the active Russian support of communist guerrillas in the north of the country.

On March 12, 1947, President Truman asked Congress to endorse a program of aid to Greece and Turkey to protect them from Soviet pressure.[7] This proposal, which became known as the Truman Doctrine, formed the initial basis of containment in the Middle East. Congress subsequently authorized an expenditure of $400 million for Greece and Turkey, and agreements extending financial assistance to these countries were concluded on June 20 and July 12, 1947, respectively.

Middle East in World Politics: A Study in Contemporary International Relations, ed. Tareq Y. Ismael (Syracuse, NY: Syracuse University Press, 1974), p. 127.

7. George Lenczowski, *The Middle East in World Affairs* (Ithaca, NY: Cornell University Press, 1980), p. 136.

A more comprehensive and institutionalized approach to containment was introduced during the last years of the Truman administration. In 1950, overtures were made to several Middle East countries to join with the United States in forming a "Middle East Command." Egypt, which was to be the linchpin of the system, refused, and a number of other Arab countries adopted a similar neutralist position.[8] This type of nonalignment has been defined by Fayez Sayegh as a "refusal to view international life . . . from the perspective of the cold war." More specifically, it was based on an "endeavor to balance . . . relations with both cold-war blocs whenever possible, and, in any case, avoid exclusiveness of ties with either bloc."[9] This negative reaction to the first U.S. alignment proposal was an early signal that there was a resistance in the Middle East to being drawn into the tactical maneuvers of the superpowers, particularly if they did not show any deference to regional needs.

The Eisenhower administration pursued the idea of establishing a system of American-sponsored alignments in the Middle East with particular vigor. Secretary of State John Foster Dulles reinterpreted containment as an aggressive encirclement strategy. The basic objective was to build a series of interlocking alliances along the peripheries of the Soviet Union. In the Middle East the plan was to establish a link between NATO in Europe and SEATO in the Far East by drawing countries friendly to the West and suspicious of the Soviet Union into a common security system.

The Northern Tier countries were the most amenable to aligning with the West because of their recent experience with Soviet intrusion. They were therefore targeted as future participants in a scheme designed to establish a Middle East alliance system. The guiding principle was to draw Turkey, which was a member of NATO, and Pakistan, which had joined SEATO, into an alignment that also included Iran and Iraq. Since Iran was already

8. *Ibid.*, p. 795.
9. Fayez Sayegh, ed., *The Dynamics of Neutralism in the Arab World: A Symposium* (San Francisco, CA: Chandler, 1964), pp. 5, 65.

close to the United States, the main task was to bring Iraq into the system. The Iraqis sought to terminate their 1930 treaty with Great Britain, and to facilitate the completion of the alliance network. London agreed to cancel the treaty if Iraq consented to join the U.K. in a broader security arrangement with Turkey.[10]

The resulting Anglo-Iraqi accord led to the Baghdad Pact, which began with a five-year defense treaty concluded by Turkey and Iraq on February 24, 1955. Great Britain, Pakistan, and Iran joined the alignment a year later, converting the original bilateral agreement into the officially entitled Pact of Mutual Cooperation.[11] Though the United States was not a member, the Pact had been engineered by Dulles and the U.S. was represented on various committees of the alliance. Washington also remained the driving force behind the whole arrangement.

The Baghdad Pact added nothing substantial to the existing American security arrangements in the Northern Tier, and was quite ineffective in bringing the Arab world into the American Middle East alignment system. The adherence of Iraq did not entice other Arab states into the Pact, and in any event lasted only until the 1958 revolution. With the withdrawal of Iraq in the summer 1958, the alliance system was renamed the Central Treaty Organization (CENTO), but in the forthcoming years it gradually became a dead letter.

More important, at the very time the United States was concentrating on building this security network on the Soviet Union's southwestern periphery, Moscow was achieving remarkable success in bypassing the Northern Tier and establishing significant positions of strength in the Arab sector to the south, especially in Egypt. By contrast, U.S. relations with Egypt in particular and with the Arab world in general were deteriorating seriously, despite Eisenhower's intervention on Egypt's side in the Suez crisis.

The Eisenhower Doctrine was another aspect of the U.S. at-

10. William R. Polk, *The United States and the Arab World,* 3rd ed. (Cambridge, MA: Harvard University Press, 1975), p. 231.
11. See text in Hurewitz, 2: 390–91.

tempt to provide a protective shield against the Soviets in the Middle East. On January 5, 1957, the president asked Congress to authorize economic and military assistance to any country in the area that requested it, and to approve the employment of American troops to protect the indigenous states "against armed aggression from any nation controlled by international communism."[12] Congress passed legislation in favor of the president's proposal on March 9, 1957, formalizing the Eisenhower Doctrine. Though implemented in Lebanon in 1958, the new policy had little meaning for countries such as Egypt, which had received substantial aid from the Soviet Union. For many of the Arab states, toward which the Doctrine was directed, Israel represented a far greater threat than international communism.

The main shortcoming of the Eisenhower Doctrine was that it focused almost exclusively on the American preoccupation with the Cold War. It demonstrated little interest in the concerns and aspirations of the Arab countries, and in this respect stood in sharp contrast to Soviet policy, which expressed considerable sympathy with the Arab position in the conflict with Israel and took steps to provide material assistance.

By the end of the Eisenhower era, the American relationship to the Middle East in general and the Arab world in particular was ambiguous and undefined. Attempts to bring key countries into a carefully orchestrated U.S. security system had foundered in the absence of a coherent procedural doctrine and a realistic regional approach. Washington seldom considered the prevailing mood in the indigenous societies or the political constraints with which the established regimes had to cope, and this neglect was unfortunately compounded by an intolerance for any signs of neutralism or unwillingness to accommodate the requirements of U.S. policy. As a result, relations with Egypt and a number of other Arab countries were allowed to deteriorate, precluding the successful evolution of an effective alliance network.

12. *Lenczowski,* p. 797.

President Kennedy never really tried to construct an alternate system of alignments or to repair the one that was passed on to him, preferring to emphasize the stabilization strategy. Johnson was also disinclined to resuscitate the by then foundering security network. Gradually he developed a different focus, one that concentrated on the Israeli connection.

During the first two postwar decades, the United States made relatively insubstantial progress on its designated tasks in the Middle East: promoting peace and stability, and enlisting regional partners to help strengthen its position against the Soviets. The "territorial integrity" formula never worked as a stabilizing influence, and almost no headway was made in addressing the underlying issues of the Arab-Israeli conflict. The alliance approach to constructing useful alignments was in the final analysis counterproductive in this particular regional context. It failed to achieve functional utility with the states that were willing to cooperate, and it further alienated those that were not, driving some of them into the Soviet security system.

After the mid-1960s, American Middle East policy entered a different phase. It was characterized by different approaches to the same tactical undertakings, often producing more dramatic results. Yet its contribution to the broad objectives of checking the Russians and maintaining access to facilities and resources was mixed. Sometimes these later efforts did improve the U.S. position in the Middle East, though not always on a permanent basis. On other occasions they were clearly harmful to American interests, leading to various forms of instability and generating friction with regional forces.

The major developments from the mid-1960s to 1991 were the progressive U.S. involvement in the peace process and a more sophisticated though often poorly conceived and implemented approach to developing an American security system on the basis of what came to be called "strategic consensus." In the next section, Washington's various peace initiatives will be examined in the light of the way various administrations saw and dealt with the Palestine problem. In the following section, the formation of bilateral agreements with surrogates will be analyzed in terms of their impact on the regional political equation and the responses they evoked.

The Palestine Problem and the Peace Process

The American involvement in the Palestine problem and the emergence of the Jewish state has always been surrounded by a degree of mystery and ambiguity, though since the late 1960s the U.S. commitment to Israel has been the most consistent and least questioned aspect of Washington's Middle East policy. In the immediate post–World War II period, there were different attitudes and conflicting opinions about the prospect of establishing a Jewish state to replace the British mandate in Palestine. To a much lesser extent, the subject continued to be controversial after the creation of Israel. Yet in time, what came to be known as the "special relationship" between the United States and Israel was given priority over most other American interests in the Middle East.

Among the principal reasons for the unusual closeness of the U.S. and Israel is the general familiarity with Jews that exists in America. Jews have a high visibility in U.S. domestic affairs and are an integrated part of the society. They are also deeply involved in the political process, either directly or through funding various campaigns for public office. AIPAC and the other organizations that make up the Israeli lobby play a powerful role in Washington on behalf of Jewish interests.

In foreign policy, the lobbyists work to persuade or pressure the executive and legislative branches to support Israel both politically and by extending economic and military aid. This task is made easier by the fact that U.S. policy-makers have perceived the Israeli connection as a low-cost benefit, one that may have placed American-Arab relations in some jeopardy but always fell short of producing a damaging rupture with an Arab country.

Political activity on behalf of Jewish statehood began in the

United States during World War II. The World Zionist Organization had shifted its international headquarters from London to Washington and New York following the 1939 breach with the British over restrictions on Jewish immigration into Palestine. The American Zionist Emergency Council presided over a broadly based project to promote the cause of Jewish statehood throughout the political system and among influential elements in the private sector, such as religious organizations, labor unions, and the media.

President Franklin D. Roosevelt tried to resist the influence of this intense public relations campaign, and some of his close advisors noticed his annoyance over Zionist efforts to enlist support for postwar Jewish statehood.[13] He made some effort to achieve a moratorium on the Palestine controversy in 1943, and leaned toward the idea of a joint Arab-Jewish settlement of the problem. In this connection, he sought the cooperation of Saudi Arabia's King Abdul Aziz Ibn Saud. He finally met with Ibn Saud on an American warship moored in the Suez Canal following the Yalta Conference of February 4–11, 1945. The meeting was so productive from Roosevelt's point of view that he was prompted to write the Saudi monarch on April 5, assuring him of his "desire that no decision be taken with respect to the basic situation in [Palestine] without full consultation with both Arabs and Jews . . . I would take no action . . . which might prove hostile to the Arab people."[14]

Roosevelt wanted the United States to play a role in the determination of Palestine's future, but he sought to preserve an image of impartiality by not announcing any concrete American position or goal.[15] Though he had made statements deferential

13. Dan Tschirgi, The Politics of Indecision: Origins and Implications of American Involvement with the Palestine Problem (New York: Praeger, 1983), p. 75.

14. George Kirk, Survey of International Affairs, 1939–1946: The Middle East in the War, ed. Arnold Toynbee (London: Royal Institute of International Affairs and Oxford University Press, 1953), p. 328.

15. Tschirgi, pp. 117, 119.

to Zionism in the 1944 presidential campaign, his real concern was to make sure that the U.S. would have a free hand in all aspects of the postwar reconstruction by avoiding partisan involvement in regional disputes.

Roosevelt's death a week after his letter to Ibn Saud brought an end to this brief attempt to establish unquestioned American neutrality on the Palestine issue. Though his successor, Harry S. Truman, was not really disposed to favor one side over the other, he was more vulnerable to Zionist pressure than the more prestigious Roosevelt. He was also deeply moved by the plight of Europe's displaced Jews. His feelings in this regard are recorded in his memoirs: "I have always been disturbed by the tragedy of people who have been made victims of intolerance and fanaticism because of their race, color, or religion. These things should not be possible in a civilized society."[16]

Truman's sympathy for displaced Jewry inclined him to separate the Jewish refugee problem and the political issue at stake in postwar Palestine. Though his marked liberalism led him to assist the refugees in seeking refuge in Palestine, he also wanted to follow Roosevelt's example of impartiality. As a result, he occasionally adopted incompatible courses of action. In 1946 he endorsed the Anglo-American Committee of Inquiry proposal that one hundred thousand Jews be allowed immediate admission into Palestine, requiring an amendment of the 1939 British regulations. Yet he also initially opposed the Jewish statehood project, preferring the binational idea that was being forwarded by Judah L. Magnes. Although he took an interest in "the operational level of the Palestine problem," or the promotion of Jewish immigration into the country as a partial solution to the displaced persons issue, he carefully avoided even discussing the political future of Palestine.[17]

16. *Memoirs by Harry S. Truman,* 2 vols. (Garden City, NY: Doubleday, 1956), 2 *(Years of Trial and Hope):* 132.

17. Zvi Granin, *Truman, American Jewry, and Israel* (New York: Holmes and Meier, 1979), p. 76.

Truman never seems to have grasped the fact that the Zionists looked at the whole question from the opposite perspective. For them, the matter of resettling Jewish refugees was secondary to the establishment of a Jewish state in the Holy Land. They wanted to direct the flow of refugees to Palestine simply to increase the number of Jews there and enhance the claim to statehood, even to the extent of obstructing schemes to settle them elsewhere. Morris L. Ernst, who had been appointed by Roosevelt during the war to help plan the resettlement of Jewish displaced persons in countries throughout the world that could be persuaded to accept them, was shocked to discover that Zionists were actively trying to impede his efforts. "At one dinner party," he recounts, "I was openly accused to furthering this plan of freer immigration [of Jews to various countries] in order to undermine political Zionism."[18]

Despite the very different ways in which Truman and the Zionists looked at the Jewish refugee problem and the Palestine question, the president was gradually drawn into support of the Zionist statehood objective. As mentioned earlier, his own preference was binationalism, which was the main proposal in the Anglo-American Committee's report of May 1, 1946. He also liked the idea of establishing autonomous Arab and Jewish cantons in a federated Palestine, which was outlined in the subsequent Morrison-Grady Plan. Yet in the context of the November 1946 Congressional election campaigns, he cautiously endorsed the idea of partitioning Palestine. He did this at the request of leading Democratic candidates in a speech delivered on Yom Kippur.

Truman had agreed with Loy Henderson, Director of the State Department's Office of Near Eastern and African Affairs (NEA), that the Palestine issue should be removed from domestic politics, and that the creation of a Jewish state in Palestine would

18. Morris L. Ernst, *So Far So Good* (New York: Harper and Brothers, 1948), pp. 176–77.

probably destabilize the Middle East and facilitate Soviet intrusion into the area. Yet the political pressures surrounding the November 1946 elections persuaded him to make a public statement on behalf of partition. Alarmed at the Zionists' success in influencing the president and Congress in favor of Jewish statehood, NEA continued to encourage an Arab-Jewish solution in conformity with United Nations principles.[19]

When the U.N. General Assembly debated the partition proposal of the United Nations Special Committee on Palestine (UNSCOP), Truman instructed the American delegation to work actively to ensure the two-thirds majority required to give the partition idea some kind of legal sanction.[20] This instruction, combined with the Soviet support of the plan, assured its ultimate adoption by the needed vote.

The paradox surrounding Truman's shift away from his original preference for a binational solution was that the overwhelming majority of his foreign policy and national security advisors, including those in the State Department, were opposed to Jewish statehood.[21] According to Steven Spiegel, the dominant preoccupation with the emerging Cold War imposed such a low priority on the Palestine issue that Truman was receptive to the various arguments about the matter and easily moved by persuasive presentations.[22] It was in this context that a number of persons, ranging from members of the White House staff to leading representatives of the Zionist movement to personal friends, exercised a decisive influence on the president's thinking.

Among the presidential advisors on the White House staff, Clark Clifford, David Niles, Robert Nathan, and Herbert Swope were the most active in persuading Truman to favor partition and

19. Granin, p. 115.   20. *Ibid.*, p. 143.
21. Steven L. Spiegel, *The Other Arab-Israeli Conflict: Making America's Middle East Policy, From Truman to Reagan* (Chicago: University of Chicago Press, 1985), pp. 17–18.
22. *Ibid.*, p. 19.

the establishment of a Jewish state. Clifford and Niles were particularly sensitive to the impact of decisions concerning the Palestine issue on domestic politics.[23] As presidential assistant for minority groups, Niles was especially conscious of and vulnerable to the pressures exerted on the political system by the Zionists. When Loy Henderson succeeded in placing the pro-Arab ambassador to Iraq, George Wadsworth, in the U.S. delegation to the United Nations as advisor on Palestine, the Zionists pressured Niles to bring about the appointment of General John H. Hildring, who sympathized with the Jewish statehood project, as the liaison between the delegation and the White House.[24] This ultimately proved to be a significant development when Hildring helped stimulate the delegation's activity to secure the needed two-thirds majority vote in the General Assembly favoring partition.

At the United Nations, the straw votes taken in the General Assembly on November 22 and 26, 1947, indicated that fewer than two-thirds of the member states were pledged to support partition. The Zionists, operating largely through American channels, exerted various kinds of pressure on the delegations of Haiti, Liberia, the Philippines, China, Ethiopia, and Greece, all of which had shown opposition to partition.[25] When the deadline for a final vote arrived on November 29, all these countries except Greece had agreed either to vote for partition or to abstain, assuring a more than two-thirds majority in favor of a two-state solution in Palestine.

Chaim Weizmann, leader of the World Zionist Organization, and two of the most active American Zionists, Rabbis Stephen Wise and Abba Hillel Silver, had constant access to Truman and exercised an important degree of influence on him. Their efforts were reinforced by visits to the White House of such prominent American Zionist sympathizers as Supreme Court Justice Felix

23. Eveland, p. 6on.   24. Granin, pp. 126–27.
25. Kermit Roosevelt, "The Partition of Palestine: A Lesson in Pressure Politics," *Middle East Journal*, January 1948, p. 14.

Frankfurter, who had played a key political role in the early years of the Zionist movement.

Among Truman's personal acquaintances, Eddie Jacobson, a former partner and lifelong friend, exercised a special influence on the president. As an American Jew who sympathized with the statehood project, Jacobson intervened on behalf of Weizmann in March 1948 after Weizmann had been denied an interview with Truman in accordance with the president's desire to avoid political pressure on the Palestine issue in the wake of the General Assembly's vote in favor of partition. Jacobson, who had easy access to the White House, pleaded with Truman to receive Weizmann. He pointed out that Weizmann was to him the same kind of hero that Andrew Jackson was for the president. Although the timing of Jacobson's visit suggested contrivance, Truman was moved by the appeal and agreed to see Weizmann on March 18. The meeting resulted in a significant rapprochement between the president and the Zionist leader, and played a role in Truman's swift recognition of Israel after the proclamation of statehood in mid-May.[26]

Following the General Assembly vote on partition, there was a period of several months when the Zionists had relatively less access to Truman than before. This was largely because of the president's ad hoc moratorium on political pressure relating to Palestine. During this period the idea of a U.N. trusteeship for Palestine was proposed as an alternative to partition. This proposal was favored by many in NEA and other foreign policy decision-making positions who feared that the emergence of a Jewish state would destabilize the Middle East, providing opportunities the Soviets could exploit and endangering the flow of Middle East oil to the Marshall Plan countries in Europe.

The United States formally proposed the idea of a U.N. trusteeship before the Security Council on March 19, 1948. Despite the curtailment on Zionist pressure imposed by Truman, a

26. *Memoirs by Harry S. Truman,* 2: 164.

strong reaction against the proposal in the American Jewish community prompted Zionist activists to exercise some influence within the political system. Furthermore, when the General Assembly took up the matter between mid-April and mid-May, majority support for the American plan was not forthcoming.[27] Resigned to the inevitability of partition and convinced by his White House advisors that recognition of Israel would serve the national interests of the United States, Truman discarded the trusteeship idea and recognized the new Jewish state just minutes after the termination of the mandate.

Though Truman ultimately played into the hands of the Zionists on the Palestine controversy, he often had misgivings about the way the issue was handled and the influence events had on his own decisions. During the heated days of the General Assembly vote on partition, he admitted that "not only were there pressure movements around the United Nations unlike anything that had been seen there before but the White House, too, was subjected to a constant barrage. I do not think I ever had as much pressure and propaganda aimed at the White House as I had in this instance. The persistence of a few of the extreme Zionist leaders—actuated by political motives and engaging in political threats—disturbed and annoyed me."[28]

Earlier in 1947, Truman expressed regret that he had gone so far in committing himself to Zionism during the fall elections of 1946.[29] He never felt comfortable with the pressure tactics employed by enthusiasts of the Jewish state on the American political scene. Indeed, his own personal views about resolving the Palestine problem were quite different from those of the Zionists. In the final analysis, however, he came down on their side, thanks partly to his preoccupation with containing the Soviet Union and partly to the exigencies of domestic politics. The fact

27. Lenczowski, p. 407.
28. *Memoirs by Harry S. Truman,* 2: 158.
29. Walter Millis and E. S. Duffield, eds., *The Forrestal Diaries* (New York: Viking Press, 1951), p. 304.

that these same considerations became a recurring theme in future administrations raises the question of why American presidents accommodated Zionism initially and the State of Israel later, despite reservations they had about doing so.

Commenting on the Truman period, Dan Tschirgi concludes that the underlying problem was the lack of a clear position on the substantive differences between the Arabs and the Zionists: "in the absence of a concrete and specific objective related to the points of contention between Arab and Jew, the United States was apt to find not only that power . . . could be nullified, but also that its own policies could further unwanted results."[30] This is another way of saying that the Truman administration's maladroit policy on the Palestine problem can be traced to an inadequate grasp of the character and relevance of the regional dynamics involved. This probably was the major cause in this and later cases. Yet it does not fully explain the quixotic behavior of Truman and later presidents on the Palestine issue, quixotic in the sense that they were often unable to find a practical functional equivalent to the principles they thought should be applied to handling the problem. This elusive question will be considered in the concluding section of this chapter.

President Eisenhower adopted a similar but nonetheless distinct approach to the question of Israel. His policy on the Arab-Israeli conflict, like Truman's, was subordinated to the broader project of holding the line against Soviet advances in the Middle East, with the emphasis on building a more active system of containment. The area was assigned a higher priority than under Truman owing to the rising tensions between the Arabs and Israel and the threat posed by the new Soviet-Egyptian relationship, but neither a genuine regional approach nor an effective way of promoting peace was ever developed.

Since Eisenhower was more concerned with building a Middle

30. Dan Tschirgi, *The American Search for Mideast peace* (New York: Praeger, 1989), p. 4.

East alliance system than with preserving bipartisan relationships or appeasing domestic pressure groups, his attitude toward Israel was more detached and pragmatic than that of his predecessor.[31] In general, he was rather suspicious of Israeli motives and was anxious to develop a relatively impartial position on the Arab-Israeli conflict. If anything, he inclined toward the Arabs, who seemed to offer a number of important assets with respect to American interests, whereas he thought Israel was something of a liability. Of particular concern was the possibility that the Soviets could exploit escalations of the conflict to establish advantages for themselves at the expense of the United States.

While Great Britain and Egypt sought to normalize their relationship and the Arab-Israeli border situation became increasingly unmanageable, Eisenhower and Dulles tried to put their intended Middle East alliance in place without creating a rupture with Egypt and the other key Arab countries. An important part of the equation was Nasser's determination to form a neutralist Arab front as opposed to participating in an American-controlled regional security system. Following the conclusion of the Anglo-Egyptian Agreement of October 19, 1954, which settled the long-standing dispute over British rights in the Suez Canal, American State Department and CIA representatives became deeply involved in discussions with Nasser about what kind of working relationship could be establshed between Washington and Cairo.[32] These discussions continued well into 1955 and resulted in a $40 million U.S. economic aid package to Egypt.

In the course of these intricate negotiations, which had a significant bearing on the future of American-Egyptian relations, a disagreement developed on the issue of Nasser between John Foster Dulles and his brother, CIA Director Allen Dulles.[33] Allen Dulles sympathized with Nasser's position and was troubled by the escalation of Israeli reprisal raids, especially the

31. Spiegel, pp. 54–59.   32. Copeland, pp. 145–69.
33. Eveland, pp. 135–36.

February 28, 1955, attack on an Egyptian garrison in Gaza, at a time when that particular border was relatively quiet. He also took exception to the "Lavon affair," in which Israel's Mossad tried to strain Egypt's relations with the United States and Great Britain by attributing attacks by its own agents on American and British facilities to Egyptian terrorists. He therefore favored a positive response to Nasser's request for a small but symbolic U.S. arms package to reassure him of Washington's support in the light of escalated Israeli military activity on the border.

The secretary of state, on the other hand, was increasingly of the opinion that Nasser's policies were detrimental to the United States and successfully vetoed the arms transfer. Because of Allen Dulles's loyalty to his brother and the latter's virtually complete control of the decision-making process, the anti-Nasser policy prevailed and inaugurated a deterioration in U.S.-Egyptian relations that was not to be healed for nearly two decades.

During 1955, John Foster Dulles moved relatively close to the British, French, and Israeli positions on Egypt, and was implicitly cooperating with the three countries in the Middle East. He agreed with British Prime Minister Anthony Eden that Nasser represented a threat to Western interests and should at the very least be put in his place. He also agreed with Eden that efforts should be made to establish Iraq as a major friend of the West in the Middle East to offset the loss of Egypt to the Soviets. This became evident when Dulles began building the Baghdad Pact on agreements between Iraq and Turkey in 1955.

The involvement of the American secretary of state in the approaching confrontation between Egypt and the secret Anglo-French-Israeli conspiracy against Nasser was considerably deeper than mere similarities in policy. According to Wilbur Crane Eveland, who was an inside observer, Secretary Dulles was in close touch with British Foreign Secretary Selwyn Lloyd regarding Eden's decision to topple Nasser, and was considering active covert cooperation in the scheme without informing

Eisenhower.[34] Though there never was actual American complicity in the attack on Egypt in October 1956, Dulles helped pave the way to the Suez crisis when on July 19, 1956, he reneged on the Aswan Dam project loan that had been promised to Egypt. After the Anglo-French-Israeli assault on October 29, however, Eisenhower effectively cancelled Dulles's sub rosa understanding with the British by condemning the attack and working decisively and rapidly to restore the status quo.

Eisenhower's intervention in the Suez crisis was as close as he ever got to dealing actively with the Palestine problem, by then the Arab-Israeli conflict. Despite the heightened interest in the Middle East as a focal point of the Soviet-American rivalry, this administration never became very involved in either the problem or its resolution. The president did succeed in restoring a degree of confidence in American integrity and credibility throughout the area, but this was soon undermined by the negative response to the Eisenhower Doctrine and the untoward intervention in Lebanon that followed.

Both the policy and the action created the impression that the decision-makers in Washington had little grasp of Middle East politics and virtually no sympathy with the then galvanized pan-Arab nationalist movement. By the end of Eisenhower's presidency, therefore, the American relationship to the Middle East in general and to the Arab-Israeli conflict in particular was as ambiguous and undefined as ever. Though the president wanted to project an image of U.S. impartiality, the general perception in the region was that Washington distrusted the Arabs and was not willing to go further than restoring the status quo with safeguards in the aftermath of an Israeli invasion of Arab territory. This left a lot of question marks in Arab minds.

President Kennedy had very little contact with the Arab-Israeli conflict, largely because his presidency extended over a period when the dispute was relatively pacified. He never really

34. *Ibid.*, pp. 168–73.

developed a concrete policy on the problem. As mentioned earlier, he did try to adopt a position of impartiality by trying to establish good relations with a broad range of local states, including friendly overtures to Egypt. At the same time, however, he was disturbed by the extent of Soviet military aid to Egypt and reacted to it the same way he reacted to Soviet intervention in Cuba and Vietnam.

To counteract the Soviet-Egyptian relationship, Kennedy authorized the sale of defensive weaponry to Israel in 1962, the first U.S. arms shipment to the Jewish state. In a subsequent meeting with Israeli Prime Minister Golda Meir, he referred to Israel as an "ally," thus taking the initial step toward what later came to be known as the "special relationship."[35] Had Kennedy been able to serve as president for another five years, he might have developed a real policy toward the conflict and the peace process, but as it was, he did little more than begin to enlist Israel as a surrogate, a move that could be interpreted as a Mideast version of his counterinsurgency policy in Vietnam.

Lyndon Johnson, who assumed the presidency after Kennedy's assassination in November 1963, initially followed his predecessor's essentially noncommittal position on the Arab-Israeli conflict. Eventually, however, he became impatient with Nasser because of his involvement in the Yemen controversy and his neutralist stance in global politics. In early 1966, he decided on a policy of noncooperation with Egypt.[36] The U.S. ceased selling surplus food to Egypt for local currency under Public Law 480, and refused to help Cairo in locating funds for development projects. A planned visit to Egypt by Secretary of State Dean Rusk was indefinitely postponed, and pleas for Washington to mediate the Yemen controversy were ignored. Relations with

35. *Ibid.*, p. 321.
36. See Fred Khouri, *The Arab-Israeli Dilemma*, 3rd ed. (Syracuse, NY: Syracuse University Press, 1985), p. 245; Nadav Safran, *From War to War: The Arab-Israeli Confrontation, 1948–1967* (New York: Pegasus, 1969), pp. 129, 132–37; and Hisham Sharabi, *Palestine and Israel: The Lethal Dilemma* (New York: Pegasus, 1969), pp. 77–78.

this key Middle East state, which had been deterioriating since 1955, now plunged to a new low.

Johnson's Egyptian policy, which was an exaggerated extension of Kennedy's, was prompted by his feeling that Nasser was irredeemably committed to the Soviet camp. Israel, by contrast, had supported the United States in the Vietnam war, which was the major concern of the American president. Another factor was that four of Johnson's most important foreign policy advisors sympathized with Israel's anti-Egyptian position. Under Secretary of State Eugene Rostow, National Security Advisor Walter Rostow, U.N. Ambassador Arthur Goldberg, and Assistant Secretary of State Joseph Sisco were all partial to Israel and played a major role in shaping the administration's new policy toward the Arab-Israeli conflict.

The other dimension of Johnson's Egyptian policy was the development of a close working relationship with Israel. It began with his decision to sell offensive weapons to Israel despite the legal restriction limiting the use of U.S.-supplied equipment to self-defense.[37] The most important aspect of the change in policy, however, was the secret collusion with Israel that emerged during this period. James Angleton, the CIA official responsible for liaison with the Mossad, became a key figure in the operation.[38]

Angleton was convinced that Nasser was the major threat to American interests in the Middle East and that Israel was Washington's natural partner in the area. He was therefore ideally suited to the particular task assigned to him, that of working out arrangements with the Israelis for Johnson on the subministerial level. He discussed the feasibility of an attack on Egypt to unseat Nasser with top officials in the Israeli military and intelligence services, as well as with Moshe Dayan and other important political leaders. In the end, with some reservations and a degree of ambiguity, the United States tacitly consented to an Israeli

37. Eveland, p. 322.   38. *Ibid.*, pp. 323–24.

military assault on Egypt as a way of dealing with Nasser's announced blockade of the Strait of Tiran.[39] It was also stipulated that there were not to be similar attacks on Jordan, Syria, or Lebanon.[40]

The Johnson administration saw a number of advantages in an Israeli victory over Egypt in 1967. Washington's principal objectives were to discredit Nasser and if possible destroy his patron-client relationship with the Soviet Union.[41] But it was considered essential that the operation be swift and completely successful. Therefore, on May 23, President Johnson authorized an air shipment of military equipment and ammunition to Israel to facilitate the invasion.[42] According to an as yet unsubstantiated report by Stephen Green, the U.S. may have become even more directly involved in the affair by sending a special air reconnaissance squadron to photograph all activities in the battle area after the invasion had begun. These films were allegedly turned over to the Israelis to be analyzed and interpreted.[43]

After the war started on June 5, the discrepancy between what Washington had agreed to and the actual intentions of Israel became apparent. The U.S.S. *Liberty*, a sophisticated American intelligence ship monitoring the situation in the Egyptian and Israeli coastal areas, intercepted messages revealing that Israel planned to attack not only Egypt, but Jordan and Syria as well. The source of these messages was deliberately falsified to induce the Jordanians and Syrians to commit their forces in the belief that Egypt was winning the war in Sinai.[44] Aware that the United States might learn that Israel had far exceeded the scope of the

39. William B. Quandt, *Decade of Decisions: American Policy Toward the Arab-Israeli Conflict, 1967–1976* (Berkeley and Los Angeles: University of California Press, 1977), pp. 57–59.
40. Eveland, p. 324.
41. Stephen Green, *Taking Sides: America's Secret Relations with a Militant Israel* (New York: William Morrow, 1984), p. 199.
42. *Ibid.*, p. 201.   43. *Ibid.*, pp. 204–11.
44. Eveland, p. 325.

operations agreed to, Moshe Dayan, who had become defense minister on June 1, ordered the immediate destruction of the *Liberty*. Israeli aircraft and torpedo boats attacked the ship on June 8, nearly sinking her and killing thirty-four members of her crew. Attempts by the *Liberty* to get assistance from the Sixth Fleet ended in failure.[45]

Though the *Liberty* was clearly marked and flying a large American flag during daylight hours when the attack took place, Israel claimed that the whole incident had been a matter of mistaken identity and submitted profuse apologies. What is most significant, however, is the fact that the United States readily accepted the apologies and in effect tried to cover up the affair and prevent an extensive public hearing. The whole manner in which this bizarre episode was handled by the Johnson administration suggests that every effort was made to conceal the collusion that had taken place between the U.S. and Israel and to prevent the rest of the world from coming to the conclusion that a de facto American-Israeli alliance had been established.

President Johnson measurably altered the U.S. relationship to the Arab-Israeli conflict. To accomplish this, he shifted Middle East policy-making from the State Department to his national security advisors, who were generally less sympathetic with the interests of the Arab world than with those of Israel. In many respects, he based American Middle East policy on the requirements of Israel, which partially explains his failure to use political leverage, as Eisenhower had in 1956, to restore the status quo. He was in effect the founder of what became known as the "special relationship" with Israel, and he seems never to have seriously examined the repercussions such a policy might have with respect to long-range American interests in the Middle

45. For other accounts of the *Liberty* incident, see Green, pp. 212–42; and James M. Ennes, Jr., *Assault on the Liberty: The True Story of an Israeli Attack on an American Intelligence Ship* (New York: Random House, 1979).

East. During his administration and those that followed, what were regarded as the low-cost benefits of close ties with Israel were usually considered more important than avoiding strained relations with the Arabs.

Johnson's main contribution to constructive American involvement in the Arab-Israeli conflict was his effort in behalf of the peace process, though this was considerably hampered by the special relationship he had established with Israel. He was, nevertheless, the first U.S. president to make a really significant move in the direction of resolving the conflict.

The territorial integrity formula had done little to promote peace and stability in the Middle East, and in any event Johnson had already abandoned his own earlier commitment to the Tripartite Declaration by refusing to pressure Israel into evacuating the occupied territories. It was therefore logical for him to adopt a different approach to stabilization. In a statement on June 19, 1967, he laid down the principles for resolving the Arab-Israeli conflict that were later embodied in U.N. Security Council Resolution 242 of November 22, 1967.[46]

Although this resolution won the support of many countries and remains the natural starting point for any serious negotiating process, the way it was interpreted by Johnson and succeeding administrations helped preserve the stalemate that became the major obstacle to peace. The principal shortcomings of the resolution were never addressed, nor was there any attempt to make it the basis of a more elaborate blueprint for peace or for actual negotiations.

Its ambiguities with regard to what "withdrawal of Israel from territories occupied in the recent conflict" and the "right to live within secure and recognized boundaries" really meant may have been helpful in enlisting broad endorsement of the resolu-

46. Department of State, *The Quest for Peace: Principal United States Public Statements and Related Documents on the Arab-Israeli Peace Process, 1967–1983* (Washington, D.C.: U.S. Government Printing Office, 1984), pp. 1–4, 17–18.

tion, but at some point matters had to be more precisely defined. They were not. Similarly, the assumption that territory Israel had conquered in a war that could not be blamed on any one party should become a trade-off in the negotiating process was never questioned. The very limited authority of the U.N. Special Representative was a further problem that was not thoughtfully examined. With only this token authority, Ambassador Gunnar Jarring was unable to accomplish anything as a peacemaker.

Any analysis of Johnson's policy toward the Arab-Israeli conflict must ask just what his priorities and intentions really were. Though the president played an important role in inaugurating the peace process and in establishing conflict resolution as an American goal, he had in effect opted in favor of the pragmatic advantages of cooperation with Israel without regard to earlier commitments and statements of principle. He had decided against trying to "convert Israel into a compliant instrument for . . . constructing a settlement based on the U.S. vision of a peaceful Middle East."[47]

This accommodated Israel's policy of "creating facts," of preserving a stalemate that would postpone conflict resolution indefinitely and help to guarantee the retention of the occupied territories, or at least those considered part of the historic "Land of Israel." Johnson's policy, therefore, had the ultimate effect of maintaining the "no war, no peace" impasse and delaying any concrete movement toward a genuine and comprehensive settlement.

President Nixon's initial steps in dealing with the Middle East conflict were to assign it a higher priority and to "pursue a more active strategy, putting forward our own ideas . . . and employing a broad range of tactics."[48] In terms of actual policy, this meant departing from Johnson's close relationship with Israel in favor of a more balanced approach and a renewed emphasis on

47. Tschirgi, *The American Search for Mideast Peace*, p. 51.
48. Quoted in Ishaq I. Ghanayem and Alden H. Voth, *The Kissinger Legacy: American-Middle East Policy* (New York: Praeger, 1984), p. 33.

resolving the conflict. Nixon considered the Middle East a volatile region and opposed the established American partiality toward Israel, at least during his first year in office.[49]

In November 1968, when Nixon was president-elect, he dispatched William Scranton, the former governor of Pennsylvania,
to the Middle East to investigate the situation and make recom-
mendations regarding future U.S. policy toward the region. In an
obvious reference to the pro-Israeli tilt of the Johnson administration, Scranton advised a more "even-handed" approach on
the part of the incoming government. Such an approach was
adopted in the first year and a half of Nixon's presidency, but it
did not extend beyond that.

In late 1968 and early 1969, the mounting tension between
Egypt and Israel gradually became a disturbing sideshow of the
broader conflict, and was eventually referred to as the "War of
Attrition." Anxious to deescalate the sporadic hostilities between the two adversaries, Nixon initiated the Two-Power Talks
with the Soviet Union on April 3, 1969. The idea behind these
meetings, which occasionally convened as the Four-Power Talks
with Great Britain and France included, was to lay the ground-
work for an imposed settlement. Nixon was convinced that the
immediate parties to the conflict could not resolve their differences, and that an externally engineered solution was the only
viable alternative. The talks never made significant headway,
however, largely because the U.S. and the Soviet Union were
unable to detach themselves sufficiently from the irreconcilable
negotiating positions of Israel and Egypt, respectively.

The Nixon administration then decided to launch a unilateral
American initiative aimed at effecting a comprehensive peace
settlement. The conceptual framework of plan was outlined in a
speech delivered by Secretary of State William Rogers on December 9, 1969.[50] Remarkably nonpartisan in tone, this state-

49. Tschirgi, *The American Search for Mideast Peace*, p. 56.
50. See text in Department of State, *The Quest for Peace*, pp. 23-29.

ment took the concerns of all parties to the conflict into account and pledged a balanced American approach in addressing them. It emphasized the importance of attitudes and intentions in building the foundations of peace, and the need to sustain a sense of security on both sides. On the question of the occupied territories, it called unequivocally for Israeli withdrawal, specifying that "any changes in the preexisting [boundary] lines should not reflect the weight of conquest and should be confined to insubstantial alterations required for mutual security."

The Rogers Plan, as the proposal came to be known, represented a significant departure from Johnson's policy because of its even-handedness and its attempt to deal in greater depth with the specifics of a genuine and comprehensive settlement of the Arab-Israeli conflict. It was never allowed, however, to become the basis of a resolute American position. In an effort to overcome Israeli objections to its stand on the territories, a revised version known as Rogers Plan B was issued on June 25, 1970. The altered proposal concentrated on bringing the Egyptian-Israeli canal war to an end and promoting Egyptian-Israeli-Jordanian discussions aimed at achieving mutual recognition of territorial sovereignty, including Israeli withdrawal from territories occupied in the 1967 conflict.

Though it was considerably milder than the original Rogers Plan, Israel was equally disinclined to endorse it. This prompted Nixon to send a mollifying letter to the Israeli government, reaffirming the U.S. commitment to Israel and the preservation of its Jewish character, and ruling out any American attempt to impose a settlement. The letter also stated that Israel did not have to withdraw to the pre-1967 borders, and was not obliged to carry out even a limited evacuation until agreement had been reached with the Arabs.[51]

51. Bernard Reich, *Quest for Peace: United States-Israeli Relations and the Arab-Israeli Conflict* (New Brunswick, NJ: Transaction Books, 1977), pp. 160–61; Michael Brecher, "Israel and the Rogers Peace Initiative," *Orbis*, Summer 1974, pp. 409–17.

The Israelis still hesitated to endorse the revised initiative, and sought unsuccessfully to induce Washington to abandon the original Rogers Plan. At the same time, they managed to elicit promises of further military aid from the U.S., as well as an agreement that Nixon's letter constituted official American policy. On the basis of these developments, Israel accepted Rogers Plan B on July 31, 1970. This helped bring an end to the War of Attrition on August 7, but since there was never any mention of Israeli withdrawal from the territories, it effectively killed the original Rogers Plan of December 9, 1969.

Carefully orchestrating these developments was Nixon's national security advisor, Henry Kissinger. Aside from his principal aim of promoting détente with the Soviet Union, Kissinger was determined to put in place a "Pax Americana," run by the United States and guarded by surrogates. Applied to the Middle East, this meant supporting Israel as a key partner and delaying the search for a comprehensive settlement of the Arab-Israeli dispute. As Patrick Seale has put it succinctly, Kissinger was committed to a "deliberate policy to stall and prolong the Arab-Israeli stalemate."[52] In the words of Edward Sheehan, he therefore "contributed to Nixon's decision that Rogers' endeavors in the Middle East should collapse quietly of exhaustion."[53]

Kissinger's negative attitude toward the comprehensive settlement forwarded by Rogers and the foreign policy bureaucracy was based on the premise that the existing deadlock was in the interest of the United States. In his view the lack of diplomatic progress would convince Nasser that the only way to peace was through cooperation with Washington rather than Moscow.[54] Thus the delaying tactic had the double advantage of eventually establishing American control of the peace process and dimin-

52. Patrick Seale, *Asad of Syria: The Struggle for the Middle East* (Berkeley and Los Angeles: University of California Press, 1988), p. 194.
53. Edward R. F. Sheehan, *The Arabs, Israelis, and Kissinger: A Secret History of American Diplomacy in the Middle East* (New York: Reader's Digest Press, 1976), p. 18.
54. Ghanayem and Voth, p. 36.

ishing Soviet influence in Egypt and other parts of the Middle East.

Nixon originally felt that though the Rogers Plan could probably never be implemented, adopting it as official policy would improve the image of the U.S. in the Arab world.[55] Ultimately, however, he deferred to Kissinger's point of view that outmaneuvering the Soviets was more important than resolving the Arab-Israeli conflict. Furthermore, both he and Kissinger harbored an underlying distrust of the foreign policy bureaucracy,[56] partly because they saw its preoccupation with regional issues as preventing it from dealing effectively with the Soviet challenge. Another motivating factor in Nixon's decision to drop the Rogers Plan and rely on the Israeli connection was his reluctance to become embroiled in a confrontation with AIPAC.[57] Though this was not the major reason for his political shift, it was nevertheless a domestic problem that he had to take into consideration.

A regional development that had an important bearing on the reorientation of Nixon's Middle East policy was the Jordanian civil war in September 1970. King Hussein, unable to contain the Palestine Liberation Organization's operations within Jordan, decided to expel the PLO from the country. This led to an armed confrontation between the guerrillas and the Jordanian army, an episode that came to have global implications when the radical Baathist regime in Syria became involved militarily.

Assuming that the Soviets were using the Syrians and the Palestinian guerrillas as surrogates in a move to unseat Hussein, "Nixon saw the situation in the broadest terms. Jordan to him was a microscopic spot on the map and yet he viewed it as having far-reaching implications on the worldwide stage and on

55. Ibid., pp. 66–67.
56. Alan Dowty, Middle East Crisis. U.S. Decision-Making in 1958, 1970, and 1973 (Berkeley and Los Angeles: University of California Press, 1984), p. 204.
57. Tschirgi, The American Search for Mideast Peace, p. 59.

American relations with the Soviet Union."[58] Nixon's own assessment was that "We could not allow Hussein to be overthrown by a Soviet-inspired insurrection. If it succeeded, the entire Middle East might erupt in war. . . . the possibility of a direct U.S.-Soviet confrontation was uncomfortably high. It was a ghastly game of dominoes, with nuclear war waiting at the end."[59]

Responding to a Soviet note of September 18 calling for nonintervention by the superpowers, Nixon resorted to Kissinger's strategy of alerting the Israelis to be ready to act if necessary.[60] The Israelis did mobilize, but eventually Syria backed down and no intervention of any kind took place. Yet the American-Israeli partnership had been reaffirmed. Kissinger later relayed a message from Nixon to Israeli Ambassador Yitzhak Rabin in which he said: "The president will never forget Israel's role in preventing the deterioration in Jordan and in blocking the attempt to overturn the regime there. He said that the United States is fortunate in having an ally like Israel in the Middle East. These events will be taken into account in all future developments."[61] The Nixon administration was launched on a new Mideast strategy, one based on the Kissinger thesis.

During 1971, U.S. aid to Israel was dramatically increased to nearly five times the largest amount and close to fifty times the smallest amount given in any previous year.[62] The total loaned was $600.8 million, of which $545 million was in the form of military assistance. The clear intention was to enhance Israel's

58. Henry Brandon, *The Retreat of American Power* (New York: Dell, 1973), p. 139.
59. Richard M. Nixon, *R.N.: The Memoirs of Richard Nixon* (NewYork: Grosset & Dunlap, 1978), p. 483.
60. George Lenczowski, *American Presidents and the Middle East* (Durham, NC: Duke University Press, 1990), pp. 124–27.
61. Quoted from *The Rabin Memoirs* in *ibid.*, p. 127.
62. Agency for International Development, *U.S. Overseas Loans and Grants and Assistance from International Organizations: Obligations and Loan Authorizations, July 1, 1945–June 30, 1974* (Washington, D.C.: U.S. Government Printing Office, 1975), p. 17.

military capability to the point that the Arabs would be forced to accept a settlement on Israeli terms.

The practical difficulties in achieving this end, and the repercussions that were bound to attend Arab reactions to such a partisan policy, seem never to have been taken into account. The policy was, however, consistent with Kissinger's globalism and with his stance on the Arab-Israeli conflict. It also reflected the principles embodied in the new Nixon Doctrine, which advocated using regional surrogates as partners in a master plan to limit Soviet influence in the Middle East and elsewhere.

From 1971 to the outbreak of the October 1973 war, the Nixon administration held tenaciously to the Israeli connection, despite vigorous attempts by Anwar Sadat, the new president of Egypt, to demonstrate his moderation and interest in developing a more cordial relationship with the United States. Sadat's positive response to Jarring's peace initiative of February 8, 1971, and his eviction of Soviet advisors and technicians from Egypt in July 1972 evoked very little response from Washington. The only positive step taken by Nixon during this period was his somewhat nebulous proposal on February 9, 1972, that the Suez Canal be reopened as a first step toward a broader settlement.[63] Nothing came of this, and Sadat found himself faced with an increasingly limited number of options to break the impasse by political means, forcing him to consider seriously some form of military action.

By the early months of 1973, it had become clear that Israel intended to retain at least a significant portion of the occupied territories, while continuing to establish Jewish settlements in them. This prompted Sadat to call for a Security Council discussion of the Middle East situation in the spring of that year. The debate continued for several months, and a resolution designed to increase pressure on Israel to withdraw from the territories was introduced on July 24, 1973, by seven members of the Coun-

63. Department of State, *The Quest for Peace*, pp. 34–37.

cil.[64] Despite its endorsement by Great Britain, France, and other Security Council members, except China (which abstained), the United States vetoed the resolution on July 26 on the grounds that it was unbalanced.[65] This undoubtedly played a major role in encouraging Egypt, Syria, and Saudi Arabia to employ a war option involving simultaneous attacks on Israeli positions in the Sinai Peninsula and the Golan Heights. The resulting October War caught Israel off guard and opened a new era in U.S. policy-making.

The fourth Arab-Israeli war and the brief oil embargo that followed it produced a change in the American perception of the increasingly complex Middle East crisis. The Arab ability to plan, coordinate, and execute a successful military attack and to disturb profoundly the status quo had now been clearly demonstrated. The issue of international dependency on Middle East petroleum resources also became a matter of concern in the West, especially among the European allies of the United States. There was, furthermore, a sharpened awareness worldwide of the degree to which local conflicts in the area could bring the superpowers dangerously close to confrontation.

With these considerations in mind, the Nixon administration moved swiftly to alter its relationship with the Arab states and to play a more active and less partisan role in promoting a settlement of the Arab-Israeli dispute. Kissinger, who had become secretary of state on September 22, 1973, had little difficulty in establishing control over his own limited initiative.[66] The guiding principle of his "shuttle diplomacy" was to avoid promoting a comprehensive settlement and concentrate on a "step-by-step" approach to securing an agreement between Egypt and Israel, while keeping the Soviets on the sidelines as much as possible.

64. U.N. Security Council, *Guinea, India, Indonesia, Panama, Peru, Sudan, Yugoslavia: Draft Resolution S/10974,* 24 July 1973.

65. U.S. Mission to the United Nations, *Press Release USUN-68* (73), July 26, 1973.

66. Tschirgi, *The American Search for Mideast Peace,* pp. 76–78.

A new American Middle East policy was in the making, and Kissinger became its principal architect. Following some tension in Soviet-American relations over the conduct of the October War, Kissinger played an active role in stabilizing the cease-fire. On October 22, the U.N. Security Council had passed Resolution 338, which called for an end to hostilities and immediate negotiations between the adversaries to implement Resolution 242. In compliance with this resolution, Kissinger concentrated on convening a conference of all parties to the conflict. Such a conference took place at Geneva on December 21, 1973, but never reconvened. An interesting footnote is that Kissinger had promised the Israelis that the PLO would be excluded from the conference.[67] Though at the time he envisioned a future Geneva conference in which real negotiotions could begin, he quickly abandoned this idea and devoted his attention to effecting a separate Egyptian-Israeli peace.

Between early 1974 and late March 1975, Kissinger was engrossed in his shuttle diplomacy, a series of intense negotiations between Egypt and Israel over disengagement in Sinai. The main stumbling block in this endeavor was Israel's unwillingness to pursue seriously any territorial settlement with Egypt. In an interview published in *Haaretz* on December 3, 1974, Prime Minister Rabin succinctly expressed the Israeli attitude when he said that "the central aim of Israel should be to gain time," to delay a comprehensive agreement with Egypt until the United States had become less dependent on Arab oil and thus less disposed to pressure Israel into accepting conditions incompatible with its own interests.[68] Kissinger realized, however, that his attempts to iron out the differences between Egypt and Israel would fail if the momentum of his shuttle diplomacy were lost.

Gerald Ford, who replaced Nixon on August 9, 1974, following his resignation, tried to help Kissinger overcome his difficulties with the Israelis. Annoyed by Israel's failure to cooperate, he

67. Sheehan, pp. 106–8.   68. *Ibid.*, p. 155.

wrote to Rabin on March 21, 1975, that "I am disappointed to learn that Israel has not moved as far as it might."[69] The following day Kissinger had his final meeting with the Israeli leaders, after which he broke off the talks and returned to Washington. At this point, he and Ford initiated a "reassessment" of American Middle East policy, a warning to Israel that it should consider adopting a more conciliatory bargaining position.[70]

This tactic ultimately succeeded, and on September 1, 1975, Egypt and Israel concluded an interim agreement (Sinai II) that brought about a significant pullback of Israeli forces in the Sinai Peninsula.[71] But in exchange for its cooperation, Israel was able to extract from Kissinger a secret commitment that the United States would supply the Jewish state with sophisticated weaponry, and that it would "not recognize or negotiate with the Palestine Liberation Organization so long as the Palestine Liberation Organization does not recognize Israel's right to exist and does not accept Security Council Resolutions 242 and 338."[72]

Though Sinai II made some progress toward an Egyptian-Israeli settlement, the Jerusalem government interpreted its own compliance as a concession that would have the long-range effect of delaying a comprehensive agreement with Egypt. The American news magazine *Time* quoted an unnamed senior Israeli official as having said that Sinai II had the advantage of putting off a future Geneva conference or any other development that might force Israel to return to the 1967 borders:[73]

> . . . we have been maneuvering since 1967 to gain time and return as little as possible. The predominant government view has been that stalemates are to our advantage. Our great threat has been the Rogers plan—the American policy to move us back to the old [pre-1967] armistice lines. The current agreement with Egypt is another nail in the coffin of that policy.

69. *Ibid.*, p. 159.
71. See text in *ibid.*, pp. 245–50.
73. *Time*, September 22, 1975, p. 34.

70. *Ibid.*, p. 165.
72. *Ibid.*, pp. 190–91.

. . . Geneva means more pressure to go back to the 1967 borders. The interim agreement has delayed Geneva, while at the same time assuring us arms, money, a coordinated policy with Washington and quiet in Sinai. Relatively speaking, we have given up a little for a lot.

This policy on the part of Israel brought Kissinger's limited peace process to a halt after Sinai II. The Ford administration's response was to make it clear that the "reassessment" was a continiung process. On November 12, 1975, then Deputy Assistant of State for Near Eastern and South Asian Affairs Harold Saunders made a statement before the House of Representatives International Affairs Subcommittee on the Middle East, in which he emphasized the importance of the Palestinian issue in the search for a solution to the Middle East crisis:

> In many ways the Palestinian dimension of the Arab-Israeli conflict is the heart of that conflict. Final resolution of the problems arising from the partition of Palestine, the establishment of the State of Israel, and Arab opposition to those events will not be possible until agreement is reached defining a just and permanent status for the people who consider themselves Palestinians. . . . The issue is not whether Palestinian interests should be expressed in a final settlement, but how. There will be no peace until an answer is found.[74]

In January 1976, the Ford administration cut the proposed military aid package to Israel from one and a half billion to one billion dollars, and in other ways made it clear to Rabin that the U.S. was determined to maintain the momentum of the peace process. In March 1976, the president appointed William Scranton to be his ambassador to the United Nations. Because of Scranton's earlier statement about the need for even-handedness in U.S. Middle East policy, the appointment itself represented a form of pressure on Israel.

74. Yehuda Lukas, ed., *Documents on the Israeli-Palestinian Conflict, 1967–1983* (Cambridge: Cambridge University Press, 1984), pp. 24–28.

In his first speech at the Security Council on March 23,[75] Scranton referred to the occupation of territories in the 1967 war as "an abnormal state of affairs that would be brought to an end as part of a peaceful settlement." He also criticized Israel for its alterations in the status of Jerusalem and the establishment of Jewish settlements in the occupied territories. "The future of Jerusalem," he said, "will be determined only through the instruments and processes of negotiation, agreement, and accommodation." He asserted that the Jewish settlements were illegal under international law, and that "the presence of settlements is seen by my government as an obstacle to the success of the negotiations for a just and final peace between Israel and its neighbors."

Two days after this speech, Ambassador Scranton was instructed by Washington to veto a Security Council resolution censuring Israel for the very transgressions he had cited in his own address. The reason given was that the resolution was "unbalanced," but the closeness of its wording to Scranton's statement and its endorsement by such countries as Great Britain and Sweden suggest that the Ford administration was more concerned about possible domestic political consequences in a presidential election year from an affirmative vote or even an abstention. Nevertheless, the policy of reassessment was not abandoned, and near the end of Ford's presidency the United States voted in favor of a more carefully worded Security Council resolution that censured Israel for establishing Jewish settlements in the occupied territories and rejected Israel's annexation of East Jerusalem.

Though Ford tried to reactivate the peace process on a comprehensive level and was often willing to apply some pressure on Israel to be more compliant, he never developed a concrete plan for resolving the conflict. It was understandably difficult for him to make dramatic headway in a presidential election year, es-

75. *Ibid.*, pp. 30–32.

pecially since he had come to the White House only through Nixon's resignation. Yet his intention to be firm with the Israelis and inaugurate a bold American initiative fell far short of its goal.

Another problem for Ford was that he inherited some of the Kissinger legacy, even though he really wanted to redefine U.S. Middle East policy. That legacy was based on the premise that the highest priority in American foreign policy should be to draw the Soviets into a system of détente, while at the same time outmaneuvering them through the use of surrogates as defined in the Nixon Doctrine. This view produced a Middle East policy in which the peace process was deliberately obstructed as part of a strategy to diminish Soviet influence by maximizing the use of Israel as a partner and forcing the Arabs to accept an exclusive American role in managing the regional conflict.

The net result was the escalation of tension, renewed hostilities, and an exacerbation of the underlying problems. Kissinger's policy accommodated all of Israel's requirements, but it ultimately extended and compounded the Arab-Israeli conflict and did incomparable harm to the long-range interests of the United States in the Middle East.

President Jimmy Carter's political philosophy and style were sharply different from those of Nixon and Kissinger. He took regional imperatives more seriously and was less concerned with the superpower rivalry. He therefore assigned a lower priority to the Soviet-American connection, and owing to his association with the Trilateral Commission took a greater interest than some of his predecessors in U.S. relations with the Western industrial powers and Japan, and sought to build new bridges to the Third World.[76]

In the Middle East, Carter reactivated the peace process as a comprehensive endeavor with a pronounced determination to make it succeed. Unlike Kissinger, he emphasized substance

76. Raymond L. Garthoff, *Detente and Confrontation: American-Soviet Relations from Nixon to Reagan* (Washington, D.C.: Brookings Institution, 1985), p. 565.

over procedure, with particular stress on Israeli evacuation of the occupied territories, guaranteed security for all parties, and Palestinian and Soviet participation in a Geneva conference type of negotiating process.[77] In this respect, his policy was almost diametrically opposed to that of Israel, immediately establishing a degree of tension between Washington and Jerusalem that became even more acute when Menachem Begin assumed the premiership in June 1977.

Carter began to address his Middle East agenda early in his presidency. In answer to a question posed at a town meeting in Clinton, Massachusetts, on March 16, 1977, he said that although the first prerequisite for a lasting peace was the recognition by Israel's neighbors of its right to exist, he also believed that "There has to be a homeland for the Palestinian refugees who have suffered for many, many years."[78] To assuage Israeli concern about this statement, he made it clear on May 12 that the United States still had a special relationship with Israel that included a commitment to Israel's right to exist.[79]

At a press conference on May 26, Carter reaffirmed his position that Israel must withdraw from occupied Arab territories as part of an overall peace agreement, and that the Palestinians had the right to a homeland and to compensation for the losses they had suffered.[80] On July 12, however, he qualified his position on the Palestinian homeland by saying at a press conference that his own preference "was that the Palestinian entity, whatever form it might take and whatever area it might occupy, should be tied in with Jordan and not be independent. But I don't have the authority nor the inclination to try to impose that preference on the parties that will negotiate."[81]

77. Tschirgi, The American Search for Mideast Peace, pp. 98, 102.
78. Department of State, The Quest for Peace, pp. 66–67.
79. Public Papers of the Presidents of the United States: Jimmy Carter, Book I: January 20–June 24, 1977 (Washington, D.C.: U.S. Government Printing Office, 1978), p. 861.
80. Ibid, p. 1019.
81. Department of State, The Quest for Peace, pp. 68–69.

During the summer of 1977, Carter engaged in a number of sharp exchanges with Prime Minister Begin, who had made a trip to Washington designed to create the impression that he favored a renewed peace process. Yet at the same time he encouraged the practice of establishing Jewish settlements in the occupied territories, which he considered part of the Land of Israel. On August 23, Carter said that the practice of creating Jewish settlements in the territories "creates an unnecessary obstacle to peace."[82] In an obvious reference to the Begin government three days later, he said: "I think any nation in the Middle East that proved to be intransigent or an obstacle to progress [toward peace] would suffer at least to some degree the condemnation of the rest of the world."[83]

By early autumn, Carter had returned to the Palestinians. At a press conference on September 29, he asserted that if the PLO accepted Security Council Resolution 242 and Israel's right to exist, he would go along with the PLO's contention that the resolution did not adequately address the Palestinian issue because it referred only to refugees.[84] On October 1, the United States and the Soviet Union issued a Joint Communiqué that called for the withdrawal of Israeli forces from territories occupied in the 1967 war, the resolution of the Palestinian question in a way that ensured the legitimate rights of the Palestinian people, and the establishment of normal peaceful relations on the basis of mutual recognition of sovereign and territorial independence.[85] On October 4, President Carter reiterated the U.S. commitment to these principles in a speech before the United Nations. This was the first time since the Two-Power Talks in 1969 that the United States joined with the Soviet Union in seeking a settlement of the Arab-Israeli conflict.

---

82. *Public Papers of the Presidents of the United States: Jimmy Carter, Book II: June 25–December 31, 1977* (Washington, D.C.: U.S. Government Printing Office, 1978), p. 1489.
83. *Ibid.*, p. 1515.   84. *Ibid.*, p. 1687.
85. Department of State, *The Quest for Peace*, pp. 70–71.

Though Carter clearly wanted to work toward a balanced peace agreement that took the Palestinians into serious consideration, he began to diverge slightly from this goal late in the year. On December 28, for example, he reiterated his preference that the Palestinian entity not be independent, but tied in some way to Jordan or Israel.[86] This set him apart from Anwar Sadat to some extent, since the Egyptian president had advocated Palestinian statehood in his speech to the Israeli Knesset the previous month.[87] This divergence in policy was offset, however, when Carter made a public statement to Sadat in Aswan on January 4, 1978, asserting that Israel must withdraw from territories occupied in 1967 and that there must be a recognition of the legitimate rights of the Palestinian people, enabling "the Palestinians to participate in the determination of their own future."[88]

Carter's inability to take a firm and consistent stand on his own principles gradually undermined his Middle East peace agenda. Despite his attempt to keep the Palestinian issue alive in his statement at Aswan, his policy on the Arab-Israeli conflict became less ambitious in early 1978.[89] Secretary of State Cyrus Vance urged him to adopt a strong position, and National Security Advisor Zbigniew Brzezinski learned that House Speaker Tip O'Neill believed Congress would support the president against the Jewish lobby if Carter presented the entire matter as a clear choice between AIPAC and himself.[90]

Carter was torn between his strong desire to achieve peace and the pressure exerted on him by other Democrats to express greater deference toward Jewish interests. He remarked on this dilemma in his memoirs: "I knew how vital peace in the Middle East was to the United States, but many Democratic members of Congress and party officials were urging me to back out of

86. *Public Papers of President Carter, June 25–December 31, 1977,* p. 2190.
87. Lukacs, *op. cit.,* p. 52.
88. Department of State, *The Quest for Peace,* pp. 72–73.
89. Zbigniew Brzezinski, *Power and Principle: Memoirs of the National Security Adviser* (New York: Farrar, Straus, Giroux, 1983), p. 235.
90. Tschirgi, *The American Search for Mideast Peace,* p. 108.

the situation and repair the damage they claimed I had already done to the Democratic party and to United States-Israeli relations."[91] In the end, he decided to attempt a middle course in which he would try to pursue his original approach while reassuring the lobby that he was preserving the special relationship with Israel. What this actually did, however, was to draw him slowly into promoting a separate peace between Egypt and Israel.

The immediate difficulty that confronted President Carter in the early months of 1978 was the deteriorating relationship between Sadat and Begin. He originally brought up the idea of convening an American-Egyptian-Israeli summit with his top advisors on January 23, 1978.[92] Attempts to ameliorate Egyptian-Israeli relations continued for months, but even a joint meeting on July 18–19 of the foreign ministers of the United States, Egypt, and Israel at Leeds Castle in England produced no encouraging results. Carter decided to proceed with the summit idea at the end of the month, and the actual invitations to Sadat and Begin to meet with the president at Camp David were delivered on August 6 and 7, 1978.[93]

The Camp David meetings took place September 5–17. In Carter's own mind, the main purpose of the summit was to find a way of resolving the Palestinian issue.[94] Because Begin's intention was to avoid this at all costs, the principal tension at Camp David was generated by the incompatibility of these two positions. Eventually, the talks reached a virtual impasse. William Quandt, who attended the sessions as Brzezinski's Middle East advisor, posed what then seemed to be the only options open to the president: either accepting an Egyptian-Israeli agreement or abandoning the peace process altogether.[95]

91. Jimmy Carter, *Keeping Faith: Memoirs of a President* (New York: Bantam Books, 1982), pp. 315–16.

92. William B. Quandt, *Camp David: Peacemaking and Politics* (Washington, D.C.: Brookings Institution, 1986), p. 166.

93. Cyrus Vance, *Hard Choices: Critical Years in America's Foreign Policy* (New York: Simon and Schuster, 1983), pp. 215–17.

94. Quandt, *Camp David*, p. 209.

95. *Ibid.*, p. 193.

After trying unsuccessfully to bring Begin into line with his own thinking, Carter had to admit that "It was soon obvious that he [Begin] was much more interested in discussing the Sinai than the West Bank and Gaza," and in the end he "proved to be unwilling to carry out the more difficult commitments concerning full autonomy for the Palestinians and the withdrawal of Israeli military and civilian governments from the West Bank and Gaza."[96] Carter finally decided to settle for an Egyptian-Israeli agreement with the external appearance of a broader framework for peace. Quandt comments in his study of the talks that "it was decided to leave some issues vague and unsettled, knowing that there would be a moment of truth down the road when some of the vagueness would be removed . . . On the West Bank and Gaza, we have decided to postpone until later what cannot be solved today."[97] Behind the whole decision was Carter's feeling, given Begin's intransigence, that as the architect of the whole project he could not afford a total failure.[98] He also knew Sadat was in the same position.

On September 17, 1978, two accords were signed by Carter, Begin, and Sadat.[99] The Framework for the Conclusion of a Peace Treaty between Egypt and Israel was relatively straightforward and led to an actual peace between the two countries on March 26, 1979. The Framework for Peace in the Middle East, however, which dealt with autonomy in the West Bank and Gaza, was far from satisfactory. It established three stages for the achievement of autonomy. The first was to be a transitional phase, not to exceed five years, designed to ensure an orderly transfer of authority. The second was to bring about Egyptian, Israeli, and Jordanian agreement on the modalities for establishing self-government in the West Bank and Gaza. And the third was to initiate another five-year transitional period, during which

96. Jimmy Carter, *The Blood of Abraham* (Boston: Houghton Mifflin, 1985), pp. 43–44.
97. *Ibid.*, p. 251.   98. *Ibid.*, p. 258.
99. See text in Department of State, *The Quest for Peace*, pp. 76–83.

Egypt, Israel, Jordan, and elected representatives of the West Bank and Gaza inhabitants would negotiate on the final status of the West Bank and Gaza.

The entire procedure was so cumbersome and filled with ambiguities and restrictions that it virtually precluded the establishment of autonomy in these most crucial of the occupied territories. In Dan Tschirgi's words, "By tying required steps in the West Bank and Gaza to Israeli agreement, the framework for peace in the Middle East did much to legitimize the possibility that de facto Israeli control would continue indefinitely."[100] George Lenczowski has summarized the general thrust of the Camp David accords succinctly: "They represent substantial retreat from the earlier position of President Carter regarding Israel's withdrawal, a homeland for the Palestinians, and the need to take the PLO into account in the peacemaking process. . . . Moreover, President Carter did not obtain from Begin any formal commitment to desist from further expansion of Jewish settlements in the West Bank and the Gaza Strip and did not insist on the return of Arab sovereignty over these areas."[101]

William Quandt has commented that Camp David formalized the existing reality that Sadat wanted to pursue a policy geared to Egypt's interests.[102] The same was true of Begin, and of Carter also in the sense that he thought a partial peace was better for the United States and for his presidential image than accepting the total failure of all his efforts.

Carter's intentions were honorable and farsighted. The tragedy of his failed attempt at engineering a comprehensive Middle East peace was that he ultimately reached a point where he was actually completing Kissinger's agenda,[103] an eventuality he basically wanted to avoid. The Egyptian-Israeli peace treaty solved the least problematical aspect of the Arab-Israeli dispute. It had

100. Tschirgi, *The American Search for Mideast Peace*, p. 127.
101. Lenczowski, *The Middle East in World Affairs*, pp. 809–10.
102. Quandt, *Camp David*, p. 331.
103. Seale, p. 419.

no linkage with the other dimensions of the conflict and totally overlooked the crucial Palestinian issue. It also polarized inter-Arab politics, and played completely into the hands of Israel. This had the long-range effect of deepening rather than alleviating the underlying sources of tension.

An important aspect of Carter's decision to go along with a partial settlement of the problem was that though the outcome had the appearance of on American triumph, it really represented an abdication of U.S. responsibility for stabilizing the Middle East.[104] Carter actually allowed the requirements of Egypt and Israel to dominate the peace process, leaving the Palestinian problem to fester and increasing friction between all parties to the conflict. He didn't really mean to do this, and must have had regrets later. He never seems to have considered the effect of this on his image as a leader. In any event, after the Egyptian-Israeli treaty was concluded, he distanced himself from the peace process and concentrated on other problems in the region, especially the delicate situation developing in Iran.

When Ronald Reagan assumed the presidency in January 1981, the American relationship to the Middle East changed measurably. This was due to the new administration's different view of the global arena and alterations in the regional political structure.

President Reagan and Secretary of State Alexander Haig felt that resolving the Arab-Israeli conflict was less important than maintaining the Israeli connection and building a more effective anti-Soviet defense system among the moderate Arab states in the Gulf and elsewhere. For them, the principal concern of the United States in the area was to contain the recent Soviet attempts at penetration, especially in Afghanistan and Syria.

The major regional changes were the revolution in Iran and the Egyptian-Israeli treaty. The latter, which is relevant here, trans-

---

104. L. Carl Brown, *International Relations and the Middle East: Old Rules, Dangerous Game* (Princeton, NJ: Princeton University Press, 1984), pp. 273–74.

formed the Arab-Israeli conflict in two important ways.[105] In the early 1980s it left Israel free to attempt a neutralization of the Palestinian guerrillas in Lebanon, setting in motion a struggle for ascendancy in this buffer state between Israel and Syria. Later, partly in reaction to events in Lebanon, the Arab-Israeli conflict became focused on the intercommunal struggle between Palestinians and Israelis in the West Bank and Gaza. These developments helped to bring regional dislocations and initiatives into the foreground of events at the very time the Reagan administration was focusing most intently on the global dimensions of the Soviet threat.

President Reagan initially had no specific policy toward the Arab-Israeli dispute, which had been assigned a lower priority. The repercussions of the Israeli invasion of Lebanon and the bombardment of Beirut in the summer of 1982, however, required clarification of the American position on the Lebanese crisis, as well as a statement on the broader question of peace. Secretary of State George Shultz, who had replaced Haig in July, persuaded the president to announce a peace initiative, and this was done in a major policy speech televised on September 1, 1982.[106]

The Reagan proposal reaffirmed the mediator role of the U.S. and sought to reactivate previous initiatives, especially the Camp David framework. The president called for a freeze on further Jewish settlements in the occupied territories, and endorsed full autonomy for the inhabitants of the West Bank and Gaza in association with Jordan. He specifically ruled out an independent state as a solution to the Palestine problem, but held to the principle that negotiations should be based on "an exchange of territory for peace."

Though the Reagan proposal was rejected by Israel, it evoked a

---

105. William B. Quandt, "U.S. Policy toward the Arab-Israeli Conflict," in *The Middle East: Ten Years after Camp David,* ed. William B. Quandt (Washington, D.C.: Brookings Institution, 1988), p. 358.
106. Department of State, *The Quest for Peace,* pp. 108–14.

positive response in many Arab countries and indeed throughout much of the world. Its major shortcomings were that it did not go beyond the general guidelines of a broadly based framework for Middle East peace, and that it established the unnecessary precondition that Palestinian statehood was an unacceptable component of any overall settlement. It nevertheless reiterated earlier U.S. opposition to the establishment of Jewish settlements in the occupied territories, and implied that the solution to Palestinian autonomy in the West Bank and Gaza could not be achieved under Israeli auspices.

The Reagan proposal never gathered sufficient momentum to make it an effective peace initiative. Shultz attempted to preserve the image of the United States as an impartial mediator committed to a just resolution of the Palestinian problem in his answer to a question posed after an address he delivered in Atlanta on February 24, 1983. "It must be true," he said, "that one of the principal reasons why we have so much difficulty with peace in the Middle East is that we haven't been able to find the answer to the legitimate rights and aspirations of the Palestinian people. . . . I don't think you can pass off the Palestinian issue with a statement about the Palestinians and Jordan. The problem is bigger and deeper than that."[107]

In the following months, the Reagan proposal gradually became a dead letter. Washington's interest had been deflected to Lebanon, where the U.S. was cooperating with Israel and the Lebanese president to establish an order to their mutual liking. As the reactivated peace process lapsed into inactivity, the United States reaffirmed its close working relationship with Israel.[108] On November 29, 1983, President Reagan and Israeli Prime Minister Yitzhak Shamir announced after a meeting in Washington that they had greatly expanded the U.S.-Israeli partnership for political and strategic cooperation, including the

107. Department of State, *Press Release No. 62A*, February 28, 1983.
108. John M. Goshko, "U.S. Pursues Israeli Connection Anew as Key to Mideast Peace," *Washington Post*, November 23, 1983.

establishment of a joint military committee to work together in planning, maneuvers, and the stockpiling of American equipment in Israel.[109]

Commenting on the accord, King Hussein of Jordan said on December 1 that the Reagan administration's decision to establish closer political and military ties with Israel without exacting some concessions would have a "negative effect" on U.S. credibility in the Arab world.[110] Certainly, the move generated considerable pessimism among the moderate Arab states that had traditionally shown a willingness to cooperate with the United States. It was, however, a recapitulation of the tendency of American administrations in general to strengthen the relationship with Israel when the political drift in the Arab world somehow seemed unmanageable. More specifically, it reflected the joint U.S.-Israeli endeavor to establish indirect control over the chaotic situation in Lebanon, which will come under discussion later.

In the early months of 1985, the administration made a brief attempt to reactivate the Reagan proposal of September 1, 1982. This move may have been partially a response to the breakdown of the intended U.S.-Israeli settlement in Lebanon. While Saudi Arabia's King Fahd was on a state visit to Washington in February, PLO leader Yasser Arafat and King Hussein of Jordan concluded a "framework for common action." American receptivity to the implied coordination of Jordanian and Palestinian bargaining positions in future negotiations stimulated renewed Arab interest in the peace process. President Husni Mubarak of Egypt proposed direct talks between Israel and a joint Jordanian-Palestinian delegation, a suggestion that evoked a favorable reaction from Shimon Peres, then prime minister of Israel. On an official visit to Washington in March, the Egyptian leader urged

109. John M. Goshko, "U.S. and Israelis Expand Strategic and Political Ties," *Washington Post*, November 30, 1983.
110. Edward Walsh, "Israel Accord Hurts U.S., Hussein Says," *Washington Post*, December 2, 1983.

President Reagan to act on these developments and revive the quest for peace.

Despite the improved political atmosphere, however, the possibilities of substantive change in the Arab-Israeli impasse were minimized by negative attitudes toward a compromise settlement emanating from particular elements on both sides. The Likud members of Israel's coalition government and the radical factions of the PLO, backed by Syria, openly rejected the proposed negotiations. The Reagan administration, confronted with such political pressures from abroad, in addition to those that continued to exert influence at home, was unable to establish sufficient authority to transform the positive elements of the equation into a constructive movement toward peace. It was also disinclined to take a really strong position in favor of the peace process because of its own earlier decision to rely primarily on the Israeli connection. The effort was consequently abandoned.

In May 1987, responding to a renewed interest among Arab states and the current Israeli foreign minister, Shimon Peres, in convening an international conference, Shultz expressed support for the idea[111] and began to consider a final attempt at stimulating movement toward a peace settlement. Following an exploratory trip to the area in mid-October, however, no new American initiative was forthcoming. The Palestinian uprising in the West Bank and Gaza, known as the *intifada*, started on December 9, 1987, and resulted in a direct appeal by Mubarak to Reagan in late January 1988 to do something about the stalemated peace process.[112] Shultz's immediate reaction was to indicate that the United States still had doubts about the efficacy of an international conference, a signal that he was not prepared to make a significant move in the peace process.[113]

111. John M. Goshko, "U.S. Backs Middle East Conference," *Washington Post*, May 18, 1987.

112. David B. Ottoway, "Reagan Talks to Mubarak on Peace Plan," *Washington Post*, January 29, 1988.

113. David B. Ottoway, "Shultz Urges 'New Blend' for Mideast," *Washington Post*, January 30, 1988.

The continuing unrest in the occupied territories, however, forced Shultz to take some action. In early February 1988, he spoke of U.S.-Israeli-Jordanian cooperation in establishing limited Palestinian self-rule in the West Bank and Gaza. Then on February 25 he arrived in Israel to start his final peace mission. After talks with the leaders of Israel, Egypt, Jordan, and Syria ending on March 4, he outlined his new peace proposal.[114] The plan called for limited Palestinian autonomy in the West Bank and Gaza, and a step-by-step approach to an eventual settlement of the occupied territories issue. It failed to address the questions of the Golan Heights, Jerusalem, and the divided positions within the Israeli cabinet on the overall problem. It also did not add anything that could serve as a catalyst to move the peace process in a new direction.

When Yitzhak Shamir came to Washington in mid-March 1988, Shultz urged Congress not to pressure the Israeli prime minister to accept the American peace plan,[115] but differences between the U.S. and the Israeli government on its substance became evident immediately. Shultz returned to the Middle East in early April in an attempt to get the new proposal off the ground, despite Shamir's strong opposition to it and a degree of Arab skepticism over its potential. He tried to encourage Shamir's support by emphasizing the plan on its own merits, as opposed to linking it to an international conference.[116] Heading back to Washington on April 8, Shultz vowed to pursue his latest initiative, but in the end he failed to enlist sufficient support for it or to introduce the necessary fresh ideas to make it a success.

The main shortcomings of Shultz's peace effort were its inability to find a way around Shamir's intransigence, its failure to recognize the magnitude of the Palestinian issue, and its reluc-

114. David B. Ottaway, "Shultz Details Formula for Mideast Peace," *Washington Post*, March 6, 1988.
115. John M. Goshko and David B. Ottaway, "Shultz Bids to Quiet Criticism of Israel," *Washington Post*, March 10, 1988.
116. John M. Gosko, "Shultz Playing Down Middle East Conference," *Washington Post*, April 5, 1988.

tance to insist on the "territory for peace" formula that had been central to Reagan's 1982 proposal and had been endorsed by earlier Israeli governments.[117] In seeking to apply its principles, Shultz never made a significant effort to prevent Shamir from torpedoing the project, often treating him with deference. Despite the plan's original commitment to "a comprehensive peace providing for the security of all the states in the region and for the legitimate rights of the Palestinian people,"[118] it never took a strong position favoring full and unconditional PLO participation in negotiations toward a settlement. This reflected a particular disregard for the Palestinians, whose position had been strengthened by the *intifada* and the more effective diplomacy of the PLO. The concept of exchanging territory for peace, which remained the only viable framework for successful negotiations, was never made an integral part of the initiative. These flaws led to its collapse in the summer of 1988.

As the last attempt by the Reagan administration to achieve something useful in promoting Middle East peace gave way to inaction, new moves by the PLO began to change the whole structure of relationships that had for such a long time been the basis of the impasse. The change in the PLO's position on key aspects of its traditional platform began in mid-September 1988 in Cairo, when debates took place within the organization over a proposed policy shift that would commit the projected "government-in-exile" to a moderate two-state solution of the protracted struggle against Israel.[119] This was followed by high-level talks among the leaders of Jordan, Egypt, and the PLO on a coordinated peace strategy. Then, on November 11, the Palestine National Council (PNC) convened in Algiers to seek a consensus on a strikingly moderate approach to the overall conflict.

On November 15, the PNC proclaimed an independent Palestinian state in the West Bank and Gaza, and implicitly recognized

117. Quandt, *The Middle East: Ten Years after Camp David*, p. 384.
118. Lenczowski, *American Presidents and the Middle East*, p. 271.
119. Patrick E. Tyler, "PLO Debates Whether to Adopt a More Moderate Approach," *Washington Post*, September 13, 1988.

Israel in voting by a large majority to accept Security Council Resolutions 242 and 338.[120] A month of diplomatic manuvering between Washington and the PLO followed, during which Shultz found every gesture by Arafat unacceptable. He even denied the PLO leader a visa to enter the United States to address the United Nations General Assembly, forcing the body to hold its session in Geneva.

Meeting with a small delegation of prominent American Jews in Stockholm on December 7, Arafat confirmed the PLO's acceptance of Israel's existence and its rejection of terrorism. Addressing the General Assembly in Geneva on December 13, Arafat stated that the PLO accepted Security Council Resolutions 242 and 338, recognized Israel's right to exist, and renounced any resort to terrorism.[121] Unable to dismiss the extent of this concession, Shultz announced on December 14 that the United States was ready to begin a "substantive dialogue" with the PLO.[122]

The reluctance Shultz displayed in arriving at this major change in the official American attitude toward the PLO reflected the degree to which Washington had become rigid and unreasonable in its policies on the Arab-Israeli conflict. Some of the closest allies of the United States, including the entire membership of the European Community, had praised the PLO's shift in position.[123] Yet Shultz was unmoved by Arafat's attempts to demonstrate his organization's revised platform, and only grudgingly agreed to a dialogue in the end. Without recognizing it, he was in reality completing Haig's agenda.[124]

When George Bush assumed the presidency in January 1989,

120. Patrick E. Tyler and Nora Bustany, "PLO Proclaims Palestinian State," *Washington Post,* November 15, 1988.
121. Lenczowski, *American Presidents and the Middle East,* pp. 278–79.
122. David B. Ottaway and John M. Goshko, "U.S., in Shift, Agrees to 'Substantive Dialogue' with PLO: Move Follows Palestinian's Statement on Israel," *Washington Post,* December 15, 1988.
123. Karen DeYoung, "Europeans Praise Palestinian Moves," *Washington Post,* November 22, 1988.
124. Seale, p. 419.

there was some expectation that the new administration would launch a bold and promising Middle East peace initiative. With the exception of a patent intransigence on the part of Prime Minister Shamir, everything seemed to be in place. The PLO had accepted Israel's "right to exist," Egypt was eagerly waiting to lend a helping hand, American Jewry was becoming impatient with Shamir and anxious to see a reasonable settlement, the Soviet Union had assumed a constructive role in deescalating the conflict, and the new president and Secretary of State James Baker both seemed qualified and disposed to make the most of the situation. Though Bush and Baker were clearly interested in making real headway, however, they got off to a slow start and then encountered difficulty in staying on course.

The principal aim of the new "Baker initiative" was to encourage negotiations between Israel and the PLO without mentioning an international conference or the "territory for peace" formula. This led to a drawn-out exchange of ideas on the peace process by the U.S., Israel, and Egypt.

It began on May 14, 1989, with Shamir's four-point proposal for elections in the West Bank and Gaza, a nonstarter designed to prevent any discussion of Palestinian sovereignty in the territories. Baker reacted positively to the suggestion but conveyed another message to Israel when he said in a speech to AIPAC that "now is the time to lay aside, once and for all, the unrealistic vision of a greater Israel. . . . Forswear annexation . . . Reach out to the Palestinians as neighbors who deserve political rights."[125]

This rather candid expression of the administration's thinking, along with Baker's earlier comment in March that Israel might at some point have to talk with the PLO about the final status of the West Bank and Gaza, seemed to signal the beginning of a forceful American position on peace. Yet though Baker took

125. John M. Goshko, "U.S. Faults Israel on Territories," *Washington Post*, May 23, 1989.

issue with Israel's rejection of eventual talks with the PLO, he allowed U.S. policy to remain closely linked to that of Shamir rather than defining a distinct American approach designed to transform the positive elements of the situation into an innovative and effective peace initiative.

Anxious to get a negotiating process started, Egypt's President Mubarak offered guidelines for talks in a ten-point proposal issued in late September 1989. The Israelis objected on the grounds that the proposal would have the effect of bringing Israeli representatives together with a Palestinian delegation appointed by the PLO. Baker then launched his own five-point plan, which reassured Israel that its participation would be predicated on the formation of an "acceptable" Palestinian negotiating team. It also restricted the agenda to discussion of Shamir's proposal of elections, while giving the Palestinians the right to express opinions on how to make the elections and the negotiating process succeed. The Israelis sought further guarantees of the PLO's exclusion. Baker, holding to his position that trilateral talks should take place, responded by suggesting U.S.-Israeli-Egyptian cooperation in the selection of the Palestinian delegation. This not only avoided a confrontation with Shamir, but failed to extend any encouragement to the PLO. Symbolic of this attitude was the decision not to reply to Arafat's letter to Bush in November 1989, expressing his "good intentions."[126]

The two principal reasons for the way Bush handled the peace effort were his preference for avoiding open confrontation with the leaders of friendly foreign countries, and the makeup of his Middle East advisory staff just below the top level. Deputy Secretary of State Lawrence Eagleburger, Dennis Ross and Aaron Miller of the State Department's Policy Planning Staff, and National Security Council Middle East specialist Richard Haass play an important role in the formulation of Mideast policy. According

126. Don Oberdorfer, "PLO Chief Sent Message to President: No Reply Planned, State Dept. Says," *Washington Post*, November 23, 1989.)

to David Ottaway, all four participated in the drafting of a report issued by the Washington Institute for Near East Policy, an organization known to be pro-Israeli though not considered part of the Israeli lobby.[127] The report advocated a slow, gradualist approach to peace based on the creation of a conducive negotiating "environment," a position that indirectly accommodates Shamir's preference for delaying negotiations that would force him to deal with the issue of Palestinian self-determination. The similarity between this procedural guideline and the way Bush and Baker have handled the peace process indicates the degree to which the administration appears to have followed the suggestions of its own advisory staff as reflected in the Washington Institute's report.

Exactly how and why the aforementioned members of this staff arrived at views similar to those of the Washington Institute is not certain. Some of them may be pro-Israeli in orientation themselves. Lawrence Eagleburger, though not linked to Israel, was closely associated with Henry Kissinger during Nixon's presidency and may share Kissinger's view that Israel's importance as a strategic ally is in the final analysis more important than the peace process. There is no way of knowing his priorities, and he is certainly a person with views of his own. His former connections, however, are not insignificant. In any event, the most interesting aspect of the entire matter is that these advisors have apparently been able to shape at least to some degree the diplomatic strategy of their superiors, who are equally strong individuals and have their own probably very different views as to long-range objectives.

The end result was nevertheless that the Baker initiative played into Shamir's hands, allowing him to buy time in order to avoid dealing with the underlying issues. A gradualist American approach designed to produce an environment for negotiations at some future date, combined with attempts to mollify an

127. David B. Ottaway, "Mideast Institute's Experts and Ideas Ascendant: Latecomer's Go-Slow, Small-Steps Approach Finds Favor with Bush Administration," *Washington Post*, March 24, 1989.

Israeli government that does not really want peace on realistic terms, ran counter to the expectations of most of the world. It also failed to take into consideration the radical changes introduced by the *intifada* in the occupied territories, and by the diminished value of Israel to the U.S. as a strategic ally owing to the deescalation of the Cold War.

With the Baker initiative at an impasse by the end of 1989, American-Israeli relations began to deteriorate. In January 1990, the secretary of state expressed impatience with Israel and the Arabs over their failure to cooperate in reviving the peace process, indicating a possible shift of his attention to "other countries that were clamoring for his attention."[128] Though the blame was directed at both sides, there was little question that he was really referring to Israel's reluctance to agree to his formula for U.S.-Israeli-Egyptian talks on elections in the West Bank and Gaza. In early March, Baker applied indirect pressure on Shamir by announcing he favored cuts in U.S. aid to Israel and Egypt to make funds available to countries in Eastern Europe and Central America that were in need of help.[129]

Throughout the rest of the month and into April, Bush and Shamir sparred with each other over the sensitive settlements issue, now compounded by indications that Israel intended to direct the flow of Russian Jewish immigrants into the occupied territories and the traditionally Arab-inhabited quarters of East Jerusalem. Shamir became increasingly adamant about his determination to expand the settlements, to encourage Soviet Jews to live in them, and to challenge any restrictions on the right of Jews to reside in East Jerusalem. Bush was equally forceful in his opposition to this policy, and conveyed his annoyance to Shamir by telephone.[130]

While the often sharp exchanges over these explosive ques-

128. John M. Goshko, "Baker Expresses Impatience over Stalemate on Mideast Talks," *Washington Post,* January 11, 1990.
129. Al Kamen, "Baker Favors 'Shaving' U.S. Aid to Israel, Egypt," *Washington Post,* March 2, 1990.
130. Rowland Evans and Robert Novak, "Bush Plays for Keeps in Middle East," *Washington Post,* March 12, 1990.

tions were going on, the peace process remained derailed, with decreasing prospects of getting it back on track. Shamir lost a vote of confidence in late March, but opposition leader Shimon Peres was unable to form a government the following month. Shamir stayed on as prime minister and was able to put together a right-wing coalition under his premiership in June. By May, relations between the administration and Israel had reached the lowest point in years.[131] A resolution passed by both houses of Congress favoring recognition of Jerusalem as the capital of Israel only made the situation worse. What the Bush administration was faced with at this stage was finding a way to place its own policy on firmer ground without alienating the parties that must negotiate with each other to make real peace possible. One of the consequences of allowing the peace process to founder, however, was that the PLO shifted its diplomatic focus from Egypt to Iraq on June 4, a development that contributed in some measure to the subsequent Gulf crisis, since Saddam Hussein regarded a special connection with the PLO as vital to his image as the emerging hero of the Arab masses. The cultivation of such an image was more important to him than the annexation of Kuwait, though an assault on the ruling Sabah family was linked to the role he was trying to assume.

On June 20, 1990, President Bush announced the suspension of the American dialogue with the PLO on the grounds that Arafat had not specifically condemned the attempted May 30 raid by the Palestine Liberation Front on Tel Aviv beaches. Though the president subsequently reaffirmed his desire to resume talks with the PLO, no concrete action was taken by Washington to reactivate them. This led some to question how much importance Bush and Baker attached to the peace process and the achievement of a balanced settlement of the Arab-Israeli dispute. The Soviet-American commitment to a "new world order,"

131. Glen Frankel, "As Peres Loses Bid to Govern, U.S.-Israeli Relations Hit a Low," *Washington Post*, April 29, 1990.

prompted by the Iraqi invasion of Kuwait, however, indirectly suggested a more active peace process as part of its long-range goal of resolving regional conflicts.

The war between the U.S.-led coalition and Iraq that began on January 16–17, 1991, indirectly posed serious questions about Washington's future position on the peace process and on its relationship to Israel in that context. The failure of the Baker initiative in the spring of 1990 was one of several factors that helped shape Saddam Hussein's policy on Kuwait during the following months. As champion of the Palestinian cause in his assumed role as a charismatic leader of the Arab world's alienated social forces, he tried to make Israeli evacuation of the West Bank and Gaza a condition for his own withdrawal from Kuwait.

Though this condition was staunchly rejected by President Bush, leading to open hostilities in mid-January 1991, the Israeli occupation remained a principal underlying reason for the destabilized situation in the Middle East. The president's refusal to allow it to be linked to Iraq's annexation of Kuwait may have been correct in terms of standing up to aggression, but at some point Palestinian self-determination in the occupied territories has to be addressed as a key part of the "new world order" when applied to the Middle East. What has been demonstrated is the degree to which an unresolved fundamental issue can disrupt the regional equilibrium to the point that full-scale war was required to restore the minimum stability necessary for the normal conduct of interstate relations.

When Iraqi Scud missiles were fired on Israel, the Bush administration actively sought to keep the Israelis from coming into the war, a development that could have driven the participating Arab states out of the coalition. Deputy Secretary of State Eagleburger was dispatched to Jerusalem, and succeeded in easing the previously strained relations between the U.S. and Israel. Exactly what commitments he made in exchange for Israel's restraint was not clear, though there were unconfirmed reports that he may have hinted that Washington would not press the issue of an international conference on the Arab-Israeli conflict if the Shamir government would stay out of the war.

Disagreement on the peace process had always been the major source of friction between the Bush administration and Israel. It was therefore the most sensitive topic in the relationship between the two governments. Yet the importance of the peace process and of preserving the cooperation of the Soviet Union in promoting the general stabilization of the Middle East forces the U.S. to make some declaration of its position. At the end of discussions between Secretary of State Baker and Soviet Foreign Minister Alexander Bessmertnykh on January 26–29, 1991, a joint U.S.-Soviet statement was issued, declaring that it would not be possible to deal with the sources of conflict and instability in the region without "real reconciliation for Israel, Arab states, and Palestinians." Though Israel took issue with this, bringing the underlying conflict to the surface once again, the Bush administration was placed in a position where it had to make a choice between accommodating Israel and promoting lasting peace and stability by working with the Soviet Union and emphasizing substance over procedure in negotiations.

Strategic Consensus

An undertaking as important as promoting peace and stability in the Middle East has been the quest for regional partners to assist the United States in containing Soviet moves into the area. The original steps in this direction were attempts by Truman and Eisenhower to build an American-sponsored Middle East alliance system, mentioned earlier. Though John Foster Dulles did succeed in establishing such a security network in the form of the Baghdad Pact, it soon became inoperative. This set up a need to formulate a different approach to creating a viable system of regional alignments.

It was not until the Nixon administration that a new way of recruiting regional partners in the Middle East was conceived and put into practice. This approach, known as "strategic consensus," was officially set forth in the Nixon Doctrine. There had been earlier versions of the strategic consensus idea, but this was the first to be fully articulated or conceptualizd.

The first hint of surrogate enlistment, on which the Nixon Doctrine was based, was the U.S. intervention in Iran in 1953. The Iranian crisis of 1951, which had been sparked by widespread opposition to the conditions under which the Anglo-Iranian Oil Company (AIOC) was producing, refining, and distributing Iranian petroleum, led to the establishment of a nationalist government under Muhammad Musaddiq. Though Musaddiq was a moderate liberal, some members of his National Front were from the religious and leftist parties. Also, the political role of the new shah was reduced to a minimum. From Washington's viewpoint, the situation was undesirable and possibly dangerous, and an intervention was accordingly engineered by the Central Intelligence Agency and the Iranian army in the summer of 1953. Musaddiq was unseated, the shah was reinstated, and an international oil cartel assumed the functions of AIOC on a revised profit-sharing basis.

The most important outcome of this episode was the emergence of a unique relationship between Shah Muhammad Reza Pahlevi and the United States. When the shah began to consolidate his power in the country in the early 1960s, the U.S. became increasingly involved with the Teheran regime, and it gradually made the Iranian connection one of the pillars of its surrogate system.

The other major forerunner of strategic consensus was the special relationship with Israel initially put in place by President Johnson. By adopting a policy of tacit consent to preemptive military action, and then providing covert assistance in the actual operation, Johnson was establishing a precedent for recruiting regional partners to assist the United States in meeting the requirements of its global strategy. This was later formalized as standard practice by the Nixon Doctrine. Its origins as a tactic, however, go back to 1967.

The Nixon Doctrine began with the attempt to justify a gradual withdrawal from Vietnam.[132] On July 25, 1969, the president enunciated the principles of his new approach to American involvement in regional conflicts. The basic theme was that although the United States would honor its treaty commitments, it expected its friends in Asia to take responsibility for their internal security and military defense. He elaborated on this in his Foreign Policy Report on February 18, 1970. Reiterating the pledge to honor treaty obligations, he committed the U.S. to protecting its allies from nuclear threats by major powers. In other types of aggression, however, the responsibility for their own defense rested with the threatened countries themselves.

The idea of shared responsibilities between the United States and its natural partners in the global arena was translated into a surrogate utilization policy in the Middle East in particular. This interpretation of the Nixon Doctrine was conceived and refined by Henry Kissinger. It was a fundamental part of his approach to containing the Soviets and promoting détente. Kissinger applied it to the Israeli connection especially in formulating Middle East policy. Having Israel as a surrogate in the area's complicated system of political interaction was the key to the success of the broader global objective of containing Soviet initiatives in the region and keeping peace in the world. All other considerations, including resolution of the Arab-Israeli conflict, were subordinated to the surrogate utilization tactic.

The underlying thesis of Kissinger's premise was that the United States can and should seek to manage regional affairs and direct them in useful ways. During the Reagan administration, this thesis was applied to the situation in Lebanon with catastrophic results.

The surrogate approach to establishing a strategic consensus in the Middle East was eventually developed into a series of

132. Lenczowski, *American Presidents and the Middle East*, pp. 116–19. Also see Melvin R. Laird et al., *The Nixon Doctrine* (Washington, D.C.: American Enterprise Institute, 1972).

bilateral accords with regional states on different levels. The top level involved close and partially covert working relationships with selected major powers in the area, mainly Israel and Pahlevi Iran. A secondary level included protracted political cooperation in regional affairs or limited agreements with important or strategically well-placed countries such as Saudi Arabia, Egypt, Turkey, Morocco, and Oman. On a tertiary level, special arrangements have been made with the established regimes in countries that have assumed a pivotal role in the regional power structure. Lebanon is the classic example of this type of partner.

The top-level alignments were established during the Nixon administration. Kissinger developed the Israeli connection initiated by Johnson into a formalized foreign policy position that was reinforced by future administrations. He also standardized the relationship with the shah that had started in 1953. Referring to the shah as one of America's most important and loyal friends, he was able with some difficulty to establish an armaments supply line to Iran.[133] The ultimate objective of these partnership arrangements was to maintain two key surrogates in the Middle East that were well-armed, reliable, and coordinated in policy with Washington. Since the American-Israeli relationship is covered elsewhere in this book, only the Iranian connection will be examined here.

The U.S.-Iranian partnership started during the Eisenhower administration, was formalized by Nixon and Kissinger, and was preserved through the Carter presidency until the fall of the shah. Its ultimate failure stands as the classic example of a globally oriented surrogate policy reduced to shambles by Washington's inability or unwillingness to take a country's internal dynamics into account as part of a regional approach. It is similar to the harm done to the Middle East peace process by a deference to Israel that neglects the transnational dynamics of the region.

During Eisenhower's presidency, over $1 billion in economic

133. Lenczowski, *American Presidents and the Middle East*, pp. 118–19.

and military aid was given to Iran.[134] President Kennedy tried to push the shah in the direction of political reform, but Johnson placed much greater emphasis on increasing his internal and regional power, with the aim of developing him into a useful American ally. The shah was anxious to enhance his own military capabilities and because of Johnson's attitude, he was able to get military aid from the United States and to purchase on credit hundreds of millions of dollars worth of sophisticated warplanes and other weaponry.[135]

Nixon and Ford, encouraged by Kissinger, developed an even closer relationship with the shah. Increasingly determined to make Iran a "regional superpower" and enriched by the dramatic increase in oil prices after the October 1973 Arab-Israeli war, Muhammad Reza Pahlevi purchased without difficulty billions of dollars in armaments from the United States. Political cooperation between the two countries was also increased to the point that Iran became a model surrogate from the perspective of the Nixon Doctrine.[136]

The enthusiasm in Washington for the developing relationship with this very special client prevented any serious consideration of the negative consequences that might result from supporting what had become a repressive regime, despite its contributions to modernization and the emancipation of women. One indicator of American insensitivity to what was happening on the ground in Iran was the involvement of CIA and its Israeli counterpart, Mossad, with the shah's security police, SAVAK. Reportedly, both organizations were actively cooperating with SAVAK in keeping the opposition movement under control, and it has been suggested that Mossad even offered advice on obtaining information from prisoners by torture.[137] However this may be, the various administrations in Washington never based their policies on a realistic appraisal of the political situation in Iran.

134. James A. Bill, *The Eagle and the Lion: The Tragedy of American-Iranian Relations* (New Haven, CT: Yale University Press, 1988), p. 114.
135. *Ibid.*, pp. 171–73.   136. *Ibid.*, pp. 200–15.
137. *Ibid.*, pp. 402–3.

They never recognized the degree of of popular discontent and never found a way to support those elements in the country that were trying to promote reform.

Even President Carter, who was deeply interested in upholding human rights everywhere, was so concerned about protecting American security interests in the Persian Gulf that he decided to keep the Pahlevi connection intact.[138] Extensive arms sales to the shah continued, and many assurances of continuing support were forthcoming from Washington. When the regime fell, the administration and the foreign policy and national security bureaucracies were at a loss as to how the deal with the radically altered situation in Iran. U.S. interests in the Gulf were now under an additional threat.

In reaction to Ayatollah Khomeini's virulent anti-Americanism and the Soviet invasion of Afghanistan, the president launched the Carter Doctrine in his State of the Union address on January 23, 1980: "Let our position be absolutely clear: An attempt by any outside force to gain control of the Persian Gulf will be regarded as an assault on the vital interests of the United States of America, and such an assault will be repelled by any means necessary, including military force."[139]

For decades, American presidents and their administrations subscribed to what James Bill has called the "supershah myth,"[140] ignoring in the process the degenerating political situation inside Iran. The collapse of the shah's regime in early 1979 exposed the vulnerability of any policy—surrogate recruitment or otherwise—that does not proceed from a thoughtful examination of active regional forces that have a bearing on politics. It also raised the question of whether strategic consensus, at least as understood and put into practice, has really succeeded in serving American interests.

The use of Israel and the shah as the major strategic partners

138. *Ibid.*, pp. 226–34.
139. *Public Papers of the Presidents of the United States: Jimmy Carter, Book I: January 1–May 23, 1980*, p. 197.
140. Bill, pp. 403, 436.

of the United States in the Middle East ultimately produced fewer rewards than had been assumed. Though the existence of a strong Israel may have been reassuring in Washington, the largely unqualified support given to it was the primary reason for the stalled peace process. Pahlevi Iran also seemed like a promising surrogate, but the largely unconditional backing of the shah finally led to an upheaval that brought to power the antagonistic government of Ayatollah Khomeini. Application of the Nixon Doctrine, then, needs to be undertaken in the light of other important considerations.

The Bush administration has been considerably less involved in the quest for top-level partners in the Middle East, largely because of the vastly altered structure of superpower relations and international politics. It is therefore to be expected that there will be little significant development along these lines during his presidency. If anything, there will be a general discontinuation of such alignments, at least in the way they have been previously contracted.

The secondary-level partnerships have been with countries that either play an important role in transnational regional politics or are strategically located and can provide military and naval bases or access to useful facilities. Saudi Arabia and more recently Egypt have unusually close and friendly relations with the United States, but the extent of U.S. cooperation with these countries has been somewhat restricted by a lack of complete accord on the peace process. King Fahd and President Mubarak have repeatedly urged the U.S. to continue the quest for peace with greater determination, but with little success. The sensitive issue here is that American administrations often insist that countries in this category adhere closely to U.S. policies without considering the constraints imposed by regional politics on these local partners.

Despite some disagreements, Saudi Arabia and Egypt consider their friendship with the United States extremely important to their national security and other fundamental interests. Saudi

Arabia has been allowed to purchase numerous defense-related items from America, and Egypt has been the recipient of considerable military and economic assistance. The dependence of both countries on the U.S. has perpetuated and strengthened the ties.

Turkey has maintained a close relationship with the United States since the Truman Doctrine in 1947. It later became a member of NATO and the Baghdad Pact. Yet in the 1960s the extensive American military presence in the country became a controversial matter in domestic politics, and some cutbacks had to be made. Although Turkey is not exactly a surrogate of the U.S., it is generally considered a reliable ally.

Morocco and Oman have special agreements with Washington providing access to military and naval facilities. Both countries are strategically located and consider U.S. backing important to their national security. The relationship with Morocco is especially cordial, and Washington and Rabat generally consider themselves to be tacit allies.

The United States also has relatively good relations with Jordan, Tunisia, Algeria, North Yemen, Somalia, and the Gulf Sheikhdoms. Though not an integral part of the strategic consensus system, these countries have a more or less friendly attitude toward America and do not try to obstruct U.S. security interests. The only notable policy divergence has been with Jordan which has refused to participate in U.S. peace initiatives since the late 1970s. Potentially an extremely useful working partner of America, Jordan's King Hussein simply could not accept the shortsightedness of Washington's policy toward the Arab-Israeli conflict, partly because of the large Palestinian element within his own population. The unnecessary loss of King Hussein as a catalyst in the peace process was never examined as something that could be changed. This reflected the inability of U.S. administrations to look at cooperation with many of their regional friends as a give-and-take relationship in which the interests and constraints of both parties are given equal priority.

Before leaving the topic of strategic consensus, it is important to look briefly at one of the tertiary-level partnership arrangements undertaken by the United States under Reagan's presidency in the 1980s. American involvement in Lebanon provides a particular insight into how a government in Washington can become entangled in a regional morass by its lack of understanding and its poorly conceived and implemented Middle East policies. In 1958, when the United States intervened in Lebanon under the Eisenhower Doctrine, there had been a similar misreading of the local situation. Though Washington assumed that the country was threatened by Nasser's pan-Arabism, in reality the crisis had grown out of a perceived imbalance in the country's delicate sectarian political system. The intervention in the 1980s involved different circumstances, but the faulty evaluation of the situation on the ground was reminiscent of the earlier episode.

After Israel's armed incursion into southern Lebanon in September 1977, the Begin government became increasingly determined to destroy the PLO's infrastructure in Lebanon and to counter Syria's military position there. A virtual invasion of the same area took place in March 1978, followed by a withdrawal of troops in June. The conclusion of the treaty with Egypt in March 1979 and Israel's evacuation of Sinai on April 25, 1982, removed Egypt from the conflict and created what was seen in Jerusalem as an opportunity to restructure Lebanon and bring it under indirect Israeli control. One of the primary considerations in planning the projected campaign was the premise, endorsed by General Ariel Sharon and others, that the destruction of the PLO in Lebanon would bring an end to political ferment in the West Bank.[141]

Secretary of State Alexander Haig shared Israel's view that the best course of action was to neutralize all the radical elements in

141. George W. Ball, *Error and Betrayal in Lebanon: An Analysis of Israel's Invasion of Lebanon and the Implications for U.S.-Israeli Relations* (Washington, D.C.: Foundation for Middle East Peace, 1984), p. 27.

Lebanon and restructure the country in a way that would accommodate American and Israeli interests. Aware of Haig's position, the Begin government began sounding him out on the American reaction to a full-scale invasion of Lebanon. Haig then informed the Israelis that he could not condone such an attack except as a response to "international provocation." This was interpreted in Jerusalem as a green light to go to war if an appropriate pretext could be provided.[142] The wounding of an Israeli diplomat by Abu Nidal's radical Palestinian faction in London on June 4, 1982, was used a sufficient excuse to invade, and the campaign was set in motion on June 6.

The United States officially disapproved the operation, but never took any decisive action to stop it. It even vetoed a U.N. Security Council resolution of June 8 condemning the Israeli attack.[143] The ineffectual American criticism of the invasion, including the bombardment of Beirut, continued throughout the summer, giving many the impression that Washington really approved of what the Israelis were doing. Even Haig's replacement by George Shultz in July did not substantially alter Washington's attitude. The idea of imposing an American-Israeli settlement on Lebanon remained unchanged.

During August, the United States became involved in the international effort to pacify Lebanon. The PLO guerrillas were evacuated, and the situation seemed to be stabilizing. In September, however, a number of untoward events led to renewed tension. The assassination of the new Lebanese president, Bashir Gemayel, on September 14, followed by General Sharon's consent to the massacre of Palestinian civilians by Maronite militia at the Sabra and Shatilla refugee camps, led to the return of the international peacekeeping force to pacify the situation. From the perspectives of the U.S. and Israel, the most important aspect of the Lebanese political equation at this stage was that their plan to restructure the country had been placed in jeopardy.

142. Quandt, *The Middle East: Ten Years after Camp David*, p. 364.
143. Lenczowski, *American Presidents and the Middle East*, pp. 219–20.

With the assumption of the presidency by Amin Gemayel, the brother of Bashir, the U.S. and Israel began to work with the new leader to put in place their intended political order in Lebanon. The result of these efforts was the Israeli-Lebanese accord of May 17, 1983, concluded under the supervision of Secretary of State Shultz despite opposition to it by the U.S. Embassy in Beirut. Though the agreement called for the withdrawal of Israeli and Syrian troops from the country, it was really a trilateral understanding designed to preserve Maronite domination of Lebanon, guaranteed by the military supremacy of Israel.

The accord was vehemently rejected by the Muslim-Druze opposition in Lebanon, and renewed fighting broke out during the summer of 1983. Contrary to the advice of American Embassy officials, the administration decided on direct U.S. intervention in support of President Gemayel and the Lebanese army.[144] When the army's commander requested help, National Security Advisor Robert McFarlane ordered an American naval bombardment of Druze positions in the mountain town of Suk al-Gharb. The repercussions of this action culminated in the devastating bomb attack by Iranian-backed Shiites on the Marine compound outside of Beirut on October 23.

The American-Israeli attempt to impose a settlement on Lebanon then began to disintegrate. The continuing opposition to the Israeli-Lebanese accord led to its abrogation on March 5, 1984. In the face of high casualties, the Israelis decided to begin a phased withdrawal from Lebanon in January 1985. Syria and the PLO, which had been the targets of the U.S.-Israeli restructuring scheme came out relatively unscathed. Syria retained a strong, though not locally unchallenged, position in Lebanon, and the PLO translated its continuing viability into new and eventually very effective diplomatic channels. Looking back on the entire operation, most analysts concluded that it represented a notable failure of American and Israeli policy in Lebanon.

144. Thomas L. Friedman, *From Beirut to Jerusalem* (New York: Farrar, Straus, Giroux, 1989), pp. 200–201.

A significant aspect of the U.S.-Israeli collusion in Lebanon is that it reflected the inability of both countries to evaluate the local situation accurately. The U.S., especially during the Reagan administration, had very little comprehension of Lebanon's sociopolitical dynamics. Decisions in Washington were usually made in terms of unwarranted assumptions and without the approval of the more regionally oriented embassy staff. This inevitably produced disastrous results.

Thomas Friedman draws the same conclusion about the Israelis: "instead of entering Lebanon with a real knowledge and understanding of the society and its actors, Israel simply burst in with tanks, artillery, and planes in one hand and a fistful of myths in the other—myths about the nature of Lebanon as a country, about the character of Israel's Lebanese Maronite Christian allies, about the Palestinians, and about Israel's own power to reshape the Middle East . . . eventually these myths would undermine all that the Israeli military hardware achieved."[145] In trying to "manage" a local conflict without an adequate grasp of the situation on the ground, the Americans and Israelis inadvertently programmed themselves for a counterproductive outcome. The question raised in such cases is whether bilateral arrangements of this type with Israel are really helpful to long-range American interests in the region.

Frustrated by the counterproductivity of its intervention in Lebanon, the Reagan administration began to act impulsively, particularly in reaction to a series of violent episodes that took place in late 1985. On October 1, Israel launched a devastating attack on the PLO headquarters just outside Tunis. The Jerusalem government said the action was in retaliation for the shooting of three Israelis at Larnaca, Cyprus, on September 25 by Palestinians presumed to be members of the PLO security unit, Force 17. Torn between its approval of what appeared to be a bold strike against terrorism and its desire to maintain good relations

145. *Ibid.*, p. 134.

with Tunisia and other moderate Arab states, the administration responded ineptly. On the one hand describing the blatant breach of Tunisia's sovereignty as "legitimate and understandable" and on the other hand saying that it "cannot be condoned," the response came across as indecisive and inconsistent. Though the U.S. refrained from vetoing the subsequent U.N. Security Council resolution condemning Israel, its abstention only underlined the lack of a clear Middle East policy in Washington.

A week after the Tunis raid, the bizarre *Achille Lauro* episode began to unfold. Four Palestinians aboard this Italian cruise liner, on a mission to attack a military installation in Israel, panicked when their arms were discovered at an Egyptian port and hijacked the ship. Because they were members of the Tunis-based Palestine Liberation Front, a non-Fatah faction still loyal to Arafat, their action was interpreted by the United States as a reprisal for the Israeli attack on October 1. The hijacking itself and the subsequent murder of an elderly Jewish-American passenger were condemned by Arafat, who promised to bring the four Palestinians to justice after they surrendered to the Egyptian authorities. But when Mubarak put them on an Egyptian 737 to be tried in Tunis, American F-14s intercepted the aircraft and forced it to land at a U.S. air base in Sicily, where Italian police arrested the four for eventual indictment and trial.

Two other violent incidents occurred on December 27, when terrorists associated with the maverick Palestinian Abu Nidal launched vicious attacks on El Al passengers at the Rome and Vienna airports. The Reagan administration singled out Muammar Qadhafi as the major instigator, though subsequent Italian and Austrian investigations showed no direct Libyan connection. Increased U.S. naval activities in the Mediterranean culminated in American raids on Tripoli and Benghazi on April 15, 1986. The net effect of the raids, which were criticized by most moderate Arab states and U.S. allies in Europe, was to create the impression that Washington was so preoccupied with terrorists that it could not formulate an effective way of dealing with terrorism's underlying causes. The way all these incidents were handled demonstrated the marked inability of the administration to cope with the radical elements in the regional equation. Reagan's policy on Iranian harassment of shipping in the Persian Gulf in 1987–88 seemed equally impulsive to some, though in many respects it was a logical application of the Carter Doctrine.[146] The president took a personal interest in the problem, and before it was over American ships were escorting Arab tankers permitted to fly the American flag and a number of armed encounters took place between U.S. and Iranian naval vessels. Though the manner in which the administration dealt with this blowup in the Gulf may have been acceptable within the bounds of established policy, however, it was based more on reactive decision-making than on a clearly thought out game plan for the region as a whole.

Circumstances rendered the original concept of strategic consensus obsolete for President Bush. The dramatic breakup of the Cold War that gathered momentum at the beginning of his presidency transformed the traditional rivalry with the Soviet Union into an increasingly cooperative relationship between the superpowers. Indirectly, this had the effect of shifting attention to regional dislocations in the Middle East and elsewhere.

The Iraqi invasion of Kuwait on August 2, 1990, inaugurated a disruption of the region's stability in a way that stood in sharp contrast to the spirit of mutual accommodation that marked the Soviet-American rapprochement. Encouraged by strong Soviet and international opposition to Saddam Hussein's action, Bush decided on swift military intervention to protect Saudi Arabia and the other Gulf states from further attacks by Iraq. Despite the adverse repercussions that armed American involvement was bound to produce, the president regarded the move as essential to the stabilization of the region in the context of a rapidly changing international political structure.

146. Lenczowski, *American Presidents and the Middle East*, pp. 243–54.

At their meeting in Helsinki on September 9, 1990, Bush and Gorbachev established a common front in behalf of what both considered a "new world order." Thus the earlier attempts of the superpowers to improve their respective positions in the Middle East by using surrogates were essentially replaced by a joint policy designed to preserve regional stability and the security of the Persian Gulf. Yet the way the United States would adjust its relationship with Israel to ensure a more effective approach to Arab-Israeli peace after the war against Iraq remained uncertain.

Contradictions in American Policy

American Middle East policy has been seriously disadvantaged by the contradictions implicit in its formulation and execution. The problem started with the Truman administration and has remained unresolved to the present. The contradictions themselves include the discrepancy between intent and actual practice, the underlying conflict between globalism and regionalism, and the inherent incompatibilities between promoting the peace process and establishing a security system based on strategic consensus.

Many of the American presidents who have held office since 1945 have genuinely wanted to avoid taking partisan positions on regional conflicts by favoring one side over the other. Presidents Truman, Eisenhower, Nixon, Ford, Carter, and Bush periodically made it clear in public or privately that they did not want Israel to have undue influence over U.S. decision-making on the Middle East. They were conscious, as Roosevelt had been before them, of the detrimental effects that would proceed from neglecting Arab interests. Even after the special relationship with the Jewish state had been established, a preference for impartiality was often expressed. Presidents Johnson and Reagan were considerably less drawn to this position, yet it remains a constantly recurring theme.

Despite the earnest and sometimes determined character of the intention, however, the actual policies that were ultimately adopted placed the interests of Israel above those of all other countries or groups. This was particularly damaging to the peace process, as well as to the American image and to the credibility of successive administrations. It seriously restricted U.S. maneuverability in dealing with the fluid events taking place in a volatile region.

This flaw in American policy is best explained by the interaction of several factors. One is the influence the Israeli lobby can bring to bear on Congress by manipulating campaign financing and other tactics. Equally significant, however, is the fact that decision-making on the Middle East at the highest level has at least since Johnson's presidency been guided by the premise that Israel is an indispensable partner of the United States and a stabilizing force. The assessment of John Badeau, former U.S. ambassador to Egypt, may have been more accurate. "In the context of American policy," he said, "Israel . . . needs to be viewed as a problem rather than as an interest."[147] Although Israel's strong presence may at times have seemed reassuring, favoritism toward it has strained American relations with the Arab countries on numerous occasions and often impeded U.S. peace initiatives.

Another cause for U.S. deference to Israel has been the influence of top advisors on various presidents. When Johnson moved Middle East decision-making from the State Department to the White House, the clique that guided his thinking was partial to Israel. It was these men who shaped and reinforced his ultimate decision to develop a special relationship with the Jewish state that included a degree of military collaboration. Nixon, who initially wanted to build bridges to the Arabs, was in the final analysis convinced by Henry Kissinger to drop the original project and rely primarily on the Israeli connection. The decision to terminate the Rogers Plan was the unfortunate result of this shift

147. John Badeau, *The American Approach to the Arab World* (New York: Harper and Row, 1968), p. 27.

in policy. Kissinger always explained the reason for relying on Israel as part of his global theory on containing the Soviets, but this may not have been the only motive. What is certain, however, is that the Nixon administration's Middle East policy was badly damaged by the role Kissinger played in shaping it.

Ford was less influenced by Kissinger and began to handle the Israelis with some firmness, though this was somewhat diminished by election considerations in 1976. Carter's advisors never counselled a tilt toward Israel, but seemed unable to find a way around Begin's intransigence. They helped him achieve peace between Egypt and Israel, but could find no way of linking that achievement to a solution of the Palestinian issue in the West Bank and Gaza. George Bush and James Baker have shown signs of wanting to pressure Israel into a more accommodating position on the peace process, but as mentioned earlier they too have allowed members of their advisory staff to play a significant role in shaping policy. Exactly how much influence these advisors have exercised in altering the administration's position on the importance of negotiations is uncertain. Considering the compatibility of what they have apparently recommended with Shamir's uncompromising stance, however, their input in Middle East decision-making seems an anomaly in the context of Bush and Baker's general policy orientation.

Though American Jews vary in the degree of their support for Israel, most at least have an emotional sense of identity with the Jewish state.[148] At times this emotional attachment appears to have disposed some members of the American Jewish community, often unconsciously, to identify with Israeli national interests even when they clashed with those of the United States.[149] This dual loyalty issue is, understandably, extremely sensitive

148. See Steven M. Cohen, *Attitudes of American Jews toward Israel and Israelis* (New York: American Jewish Committee, 1983).
149. Wolf Blitzer, "Why Did He Spy?" *Washington Jewish Week*, February 26, 1987, p. 1. Blitzer quotes Jonathan Pollard, who was convicted of spying for Israel, as having said that "there was no difference between being a good American and being a good Zionist."

for the vast majority of American Jews, who consider themselves to be loyal and patriotic citizens.

With very few exceptions,[150] the dual loyalty issue has not been taken into consideration when Jews have been placed in influential decision-making positions or given access to politically sensitive information. How much a sense of identity with the Jewish state affected the behavior of Jewish officials on the highest levels, where Washington's fundamental approach to the Middle East is determined, is unknown and perhaps can never be known. But in some instances it may well have been a factor. This must be recognized in any thoughtful analysis of U.S. Middle East policy.

The conflict between the global and regional approaches to decision-making has been the basis of the second contradiction in American Middle East policy. On the many occasions when the rivalry with the Soviet Union for ascendancy in the Middle East was given the highest priority in decision-making, regional factors generally received less consideration. This has come under discussion earlier, but it should be noted here that there is a major link between policy based on various theories about containing the Soviets, and the disruption of the peace process and political dislocations in the area.

The connection has been primarily based on the concept of using the top-level surrogates as a countervailing force in the power game. The principal architect of this approach to the Middle East was Henry Kissinger, whose legacy outlasted his role as decision-maker. Kissinger's preoccupation with outmaneuvering the Soviets, his conviction that power was the only significant reality in international politics, and his emphasis on using the Israeli and Pahlevi connections as major instruments of U.S. policy became the conceptual framework through which American administrations looked at and dealt with the area. It had forerunners, but under Kissinger it became standardized.

150. Brzezinski, p. 239. Brzezinski denied White House domestic advisor Stuart Eizenstat access to sensitive cables dealing with Israel.

The Kissinger view of the global arena has not consistently dominated the way Washington has handled the Middle East, but it keeps recurring and has to a degree become ingrained in the system. The problem is that such a focus on global concerns obscures the regional equation. Middle East policy today cannot be effective on any level if it does not take into major consideration the fact that politics has gone to the street, to the grass roots. The overthrow of the shah in Iran and the *intifada* in the occupied territories are the most apparent manifestations of this phenomenon. There is no place in the Kissinger picture of world politics for "people power" in any form. Yet it has been definitively shown that this dimension of the political equation is not only real, but often decisive.

Much of the alienation from American diplomacy among the politicized masses and radicalized intelligentsia of the Middle East stems from the inherent conflict between Kissinger-style globalism as an approach and the increasingly powerful indigenous sociopolitical forces as a regional reality. For decades, area specialists in the State Department and other agencies, as well as those in universities and other institutions, have urged the adoption of a regional approach. Though some presidents recognized the validity of this premise, they generally allowed themselves to be drawn into decision-making that was primarily global in character. This is no longer possible in the light of recent events, but it has been a principal cause of a debilitating contradiction in American Middle East policy.

The final contradiction in U.S. decision-making on the area arises from the incompatibility between the peace process and the construction of a security system based on surrogates. Though this was covered in the discussion of the peace process, it deserves further mention here. The biggest obstacle to a successful resolution of the Arab-Israeli conflict has been Israel's unwillingness to return the occupied territories and accept a two-state solution, compounded by the disinclination of the United States steadfastly to reaffirm its own preference for such an outcome.

In the final analysis, it seems, Washington has considered Israel's surrogate role more important to American interests than the conclusion of peace between Israel and the Arabs, including the Palestinians. The influence of the Kissinger thesis is, of course, a key factor in this aspect of U.S. Middle East policy. It is not possible for the United States to do what Israel wants and to achieve peace at the same time. The most basic reason for this is that Israel does not really want peace, at least not on the grounds that could make it realistically possible.

This means that in the case of the Arab-Israeli conflict, a choice has to be made between peace and strategic consensus. So far, all administrations have in one way or another chosen the latter, even those that did not really want to do so. If and when peace comes to be regarded as more important than anything else and appropriate action is taken to achieve it, this contradiction will have been resolved.

All three of these contradictions in U.S. policy have been detrimental to American interests in the Middle East. Any attempt to reverse the situation can only take place when practice is geared to constructive intent, regional considerations are assigned priority over global concerns, and strategic consensus is subordinated to the quest for peace. In any event, the transition will probably not be easy.

The change in Soviet-American relations that emerged in 1989–90 went a long way in diminishing the importance of strategic consensus. Yet the Bush administration did not prevent Israel from derailing the peace process in mid-1990 and assiduously avoided linking the Palestinian issue to the subsequent Gulf crisis. One of the most important questions in the aftermath of the war between the coalition and Iraq is whether Washington will assign a higher priority to resolving the Arab-Israeli conflict than to preserving its traditional relationship with Israel at a time when the future course of Soviet policy has become uncertain.

4   SOVIET POLICY

OVIET Middle East policy stems from security concerns related to the proximity of the area to the U.S.S.R. and from the interest Soviet regimes have taken in it for ideological and global power reasons. Following a brief attempt to establish an identity of interests with the Middle Eastern working class in the unsuccessful Baku Congress of 1920, the Soviet Union was relatively uninvolved in the area during the following twenty-five years. After World War II, however, this non-interventionist policy gave way to intense political activity, a renewal of the old nineteenth-century Russian "forward policy."

Aware that the European colonial powers were beginning a process of decolonization in the Middle East and that the United States would be seeking to preserve the Western position there in some different form, Moscow adopted an intrusive posture designed to establish new gains in this important neighboring region. The principal considerations were to protect the Soviet Union's southwestern security flank, to compete with the United States in the superpower rivalry that had just surfaced, and to create a degree of ideological affinity with the indigenous states and societies. What this meant in practice was that the Soviet Union had become a major actor in the international relations of the Middle East.

Self-Image

In Fred Halliday's words, "The Soviet Union sees itself as part of a world system that is in competition with the capitalist world system and which will, sooner or later, prevail over it."[1] It also felt committed to assisting in all feasible ways what it regarded as "progressive forces" in the international arena. Aside from this ideological self-image, it was highly conscious of confronting America's military capability and encirclement strategy, a situation that forced it to preserve its own power and to develop friendly relations with as many countries as possible, regardless of their political orientation.

In the Middle East, the Soviets had considerable difficulty in formulating a policy that was effective in terms of their own interests. Like the Americans, they were so preoccupied with the superpower rivalry itself that they concentrated mainly on a global as opposed to a regional approach. Their grasp of the socio-political dynamics within the Middle East itself was superficial and inept, producing an unenviable record of costly mistakes and long-term losses in political influence.

Although limited in available resources and ideological appeal and aware of the need to work out some *modus vivendi* with the West to avoid war, the Soviets tried to make their own self-image credible in the Middle East. The major emphasis was on creating the impression that the Soviet Union and the indigenous countries and peoples had common interests and, more importantly, common enemies, especially the "imperialist" powers of the West. Building an "anti-imperialist" front in the Middle East was a primary objective of the Soviet Union for decades.

The success of this endeavor, however, was very limited. Although numerous Middle Eastern governments and countless conference resolutions paid lip service to the idea that Western "imperialism" was the principal adversary of the regional states and the Soviet Union, there was never a strong conviction in the area that a real identity of interests existed. The local concern has been more with the fulfillment of nationalist aspirations and

1. Fred Halliday, *Soviet Policy in the Arc of Crisis* (Washington, D.C.: Institute for Policy Studies, 1981), p. 28.

the achievement of genuine independence than with involvement in external alignments. It was also not forgotten that the Russian attitude toward the Middle East has traditionally been opportunistic rather than benign, and that parts of the area were incorporated in the old Tsarist empire and retained by the Soviets following the 1917 revolution.

The U.S.S.R. nonetheless never ceased in its persistent attempts to project a "liberator" image of itself in the Middle East and the Third World in general. This was partly because the Soviets really saw themselves in such a role, but also because anti-imperialism was the only ideology they shared with the governments and societies of the area. This exclusive emphasis on anti-imperialism was in one sense a manifestation of their lack of an adequate regional approach, a viable system of understanding and dealing with the indigenous social and political forces. It was also a rather artificial and thematically weak method of developing a constructive dialogue with another people.

A further obstacle to a convincing presentation of the common Soviet–Middle Eastern anti-imperialist concept was the degree to which this notion has been overstated in Soviet ideological doctrine. It became an integral part of a political formula that much of the world increasingly saw as the sloganism of a ruling elite that in fact kept a tight grip on its own society and was as intent as the West on forwarding its own interests in international affairs. The repetitiveness and intellectually vacuous character of such a generalization about contemporary power politics detract from its credibility and raise questions as to the sincerity of those seeking to propagate it. The Soviet invasion of Afghanistan virtually ended Moscow's attempt to convince the Third World that its own policies were not imperialistic when contrasted with those of the United States, and eventually led to a new era in Soviet–Middle Eastern relations.

Self-image and attempts to portray the Soviet Union as the natural friend and partner of Middle Eastern states and societies were only the apologetic and public relations side of Soviet policy and activity in the area. Far more important in terms of movement toward concrete, designated goals were the political methods by which the decision-making elite in Moscow went about achieving advantages in the intense rivalry for superiority with the United States. Soviet policy has evolved through decades of experimentation with various tactics, some at least temporarily successful and others disappointing from the start. What ultimately matters is the degree to which Moscow learned from mistakes.

Political Methods

The Soviet Union's policy toward the Middle East has evolved in stages since the end of World War II. The initial period, which extended from the end of the war to Stalin's death in 1953, was marked by a heavy-handed intrusiveness that ultimately proved ineffective and counterproductive. Among the dramatic early manifestations of this policy was the short-lived refusal of the Soviet Union to withdraw its troops from Iran at the agreed time of six months after the end of the war. Another was the series of demands Moscow imposed on Turkey immediately following the defeat of Germany.[2] Included were the return of Kars and Ardahan to Russia, Soviet military base rights in the Bosphorus and the Dardanelles, changes in the Turkish-Bulgarian border in favor of Bulgaria, and a revision of the 1936 Montreux Convention designed to bring the Straits under the control of the Black Sea powers (Turkey, the Soviet Union, Rumania, and Bulgaria). Backed by the United States under the Truman Doctrine, Turkey successfully resisted this attempt to diminish its sovereignty.

Another aim of Soviet Middle East policy during this period was to foster communist subversion in the regional states, though no concrete tactic was ever developed. The intended

2. George Lenczowski, *The Middle East in World Affairs*, 4th ed. (Ithaca, NY: Cornell University Press, 1980), p. 135.

political action was notably remiss in its failure to recognize the popularity of the broad nationalist liberation movement and the disinclination of the indigenous countries to take sides in the unfolding superpower rivalry. The Soviets were as naive and inexperienced as the United States in dealing with the Middle East. They were particularly clumsy in their attempts to promote destabilization and make bold, aggressive inroads at a time when Middle Eastern countries were trying to move in a positive political direction and compensate for the dislocations the war had produced.

During the Khrushchev era, from 1953 to 1964, a more astute Soviet policy gradually emerged. Recognizing that the Middle Eastern states had their own distinct interests, the new Soviet leader sought to win them over through military and economic aid and expressions of sympathy with their problems and aspirations. A major difficulty in this undertaking was what seemed at the time to be a shift to the left in a number of countries, which prompted communist parties in those countries to seek a revolutionary takeover. Torn between the need to develop friendly ties on the basis of support for indigenous political programs on the one hand and the temptation to encourage communist revolution on the other, the Khrushchev regime never fully clarified its position. In 1957 and 1958, the communists in Syria and Iraq came close to tipping the tenuous balance of power in their favor, and the Soviets watched with interest without committing themselves. In the end, however, neither indigenous communist group succeeded. The Syrian communists lost their opportunity when Egypt and Syria merged into the United Arab Republic in February 1958. In Iraq, Brigadier Qassem established his own dictatorship after the fall of the monarchy without the cooperation of any political group in the country.

The tactic developed after this, in the early 1960s, was to encourage indigenous communist groups to assume a low profile or disband, allowing the members to cooperate with or join the major nationalist parties and thus remain in the political process.[3] Though this worked with some success in Egypt and Algeria, it did not establish significant Soviet influence in either system. Some headway was also made under Khrushchev in opening up better relations with Turkey and Iran. In the case of Turkey, it was barely the beginning of more friendly ties, but after the shah announced that foreign missile bases would not be allowed in Iran, Moscow approved a $40 million loan to that country.[4] Though Khrushchev had only limited achievements in the Middle East, he did abandon the unenlightened Stalinist policy for a more sophisticated approach to the area. It should also be remembered that the Soviet relationship with Nasser's Egypt, which was such an important factor in the Middle East equation from 1955 to 1970, originated during his tenure.

After Brezhnev and Kosygin took over the reins of power in 1964, Soviet Middle East policy underwent some significant changes. A particularly important development was the apparent decision to make the area a special focus of attention and activity.[5] The "popular front" tactic started under Khrushchev, which emphasized common interests, was emphatically endorsed, and there was a concerted effort to establish a broadly based system of cordial state-to-state relations.

In the Arab sphere, there was a special endeavor to promote a Soviet-sponsored "anti-imperialist" front against the United States and Israel. This remained for many years a primary Russian objective in the Arab world, though it was never satisfactorily realized. In the late 1960s, however, a great deal of Soviet military and economic support went into this project, including the rebuilding of the Egyptian and Syrian armed forces after the devastating 1967 war. Also at this time an effort was made to diversify Soviet Middle East contacts by developing friendly relations with such countries as Jordan and North and South Yemen, though Egypt remained the major focus.

3. Robert O. Freedman, *Soviet Policy toward the Middle East since 1970,* 3rd ed. (New York: Praeger, 1982), pp. 14–19.
    4. *Ibid.,* pp. 19–20.   5. *Ibid.,* pp. 22–41.

Relations with Turkey and Iran were considerably improved in the later 1960s. The Soviet position on Cyprus, which had been mainly pro-Greek, was altered to draw Turkey closer to the Soviet Union. Loans to assist industrial projects were also forthcoming from Moscow. Iran, which had already received Soviet aid, was given military equipment and other financial loans with a dollar value of hundreds of millions. In the early 1970s, an economic treaty between the two countries increased the extent of Soviet trade with Iran. Though never able to match the American relationship with these countries, these developments brought the Soviets closer to them than ever before and did a lot to end the hostility that had existed in the immediate post–World War II period.

By 1970, the U.S.S.R. had greatly improved its position in the Middle East. It had close ties with several countries, relatively good relations with a number of others, and military privileges in Egypt, Sudan, Syria, Iraq, and the two Yemens. The principal question was the extent to which these gains offset those of the United States. Despite American mistakes and losses, the Soviet Union was never able to establish a clear superiority over the other superpower in the area.

In the 1970s and 1980s the Soviets had difficulty in maintaining their advantages, and in many cases they lost ground. There was an underlying conflict of interests between their policy of promoting an anti-imperialist front and the nationalist aims of the indigenous states. This became apparent in the events surrounding the abortive coup against Numeiri's regime in Sudan in mid-1971. In the context of discussions on the formation of a Federation of Arab Republics that was to include Egypt, Sudan, Libya, and Syria, a confrontation developed between the government and the Abdul Maghub faction of the Sudanese Communist Party in late May 1971. Numeiri, who had favored the controversial merger, was ousted on July 19. The Soviets had been observing this with considerable interest and approval, but were deeply disturbed when Numeiri was restored to power with the help of Egypt and Libya a few days later.

The abortive communist coup in Sudan was a major setback for Moscow and led to a reexamination by the Soviets of their Middle East policy.[6] The most important developments to come out of this were a tendency to place less stock in the anti-imperialist front tactic and to develop a broader system of cooperative relationships in the Middle East. This became an increasingly essential step as Egypt under Sadat gradually drifted away from the close connection with the Soviet Union it had had in the Nasser years. Despite the Soviet-Egyptian Treaty of Friendship and Cooperation, signed in May 1971, relations between the two countries became progressively less cordial, especially after the October 1973 war. The Soviets therefore diversified their Middle East liaisons accordingly.

Overtures designed to initiate friendly relations were made to Arafat and the PLO, Jordan, Lebanon, North Yemen, Qatar, and the United Arab Emirates initially. Later, Libya and Ethiopia became the focus of special Soviet attention. Support and encouragement were naturally given to the leftist Popular Front for the Liberation of the Arab Gulf (PFLOAG). These attempts to expand the Soviet patronage system in the Middle East will be examined in the following section, but it should be noted here that despite a number of treaties concluded with Middle Eastern states in the 1970s and 1980s, most of Moscow's clients either proved unreliable partners or were diverted from assigning priority to the Soviet connection by internal politics and involvement in regional disputes and rivalries. The Soviets often found this annoying and frustrating as they sought to compete successfully with the United States while simultaneously trying to preserve the détente relationship with Washington for the sake of world peace.

Another Soviet concern was keeping the U.S.S.R. involved in or in control of the major developments taking place in the Middle East. This included participation in the peace process after the October 1973 war, and making the most of such disloca-

<hr />

6. *Ibid.*, pp. 63–69.

tions as the suspension of Egypt from the Arab system and the revolution in Iran, both during 1978–79.

Though the Soviet Union enhanced its prestige in the Arab world by supplying Sadat and Asad before and during the 1973 war, Moscow was outmaneuvered by Kissinger after the cease-fire. The Soviets did manage to work themselves into the center of peace diplomacy through their participation in the Geneva Conference of December 21, 1973. But when the conference ended without any progress having been made, the initiative reverted to the United States.

The American secretary of state dominated the peace process thereafter, and the oil embargo that had been imposed after the war was lifted on March 19, 1974. Despite the limited success of Kissinger's shuttle diplomacy and Washington's eventual recourse to other methods of working toward a resolution of the Arab-Israeli conflict, the U.S. continued to exercise the greater degree of influence in this area of endeavor and increasingly established itself as the principal mediator. Commenting on the Soviet reaction to this, Robert Freedman notes that "In their 'zero-sum' view of Middle East influence they [the Soviets] were quite concerned that the sharp rise in American prestige in the region meant a concomitant drop in Soviet influence."[7]

Another way in which Kissinger established limits on Soviet maneuverability in the Middle East was his promotion of détente. Responding to the secretary of state's agile diplomacy and acting on its own realization that Middle East tensions could lead to a superpower confrontation, Moscow accepted détente as a more refined version of coexistence. What this meant in essence was that a degree of cooperation with the West had been endorsed without abandoning the theory that the Soviet Union was the leader of the world's progressive forces. Yet détente certainly curtailed the degree to which the Soviet Union could accommodate the interests of regional states in the Middle East.

7. *Ibid.*, p. 171.

The negative reaction in much of the Arab world to Sadat's dramatic moves toward peace with Israel between November 1977 and March 1979 opened up opportunities for the Soviets to improve their tenuous position in the Middle East. Though they had some success in identifying with the Arab opposition to Sadat by expressing their own hostility to Camp David and the Egyptian-Israeli peace treaty, they were never really able to orchestrate an Arab front movement on the separate peace issue. As inter-Arab politics concentrated on the challenge of revolutionary Iran and became reoriented in terms of the Iran-Iraq war, the Soviet role became increasingly peripheral. Also, the Soviet invasion of Afghanistan in December 1979 dealt a severe blow to the Russian image in the Middle East and undermined any gains that had been made in the 1970s.

The fall of the shah and the establishment of a revolutionary Islamic regime in Teheran in early 1979 was welcomed by Moscow because it ended the surrogate role Iran had played for the United States for over two decades and brought to power a virulently anti-American regime. Yet this radical change in Iran produced extremely limited if any advantages for the Soviets. The Khomeini government was always skeptical of the U.S.S.R., initially because of its official communist atheism and later also because its involvement in Afghanistan cast it in the role of a great power at war with a Muslim populace.

In these respects, the Soviets were not only unable to direct the course of events in the 1970s and 1980s, but were often overrun by them. They were ultimately unable to establish either a political alignment or an anti-imperialist front, and had the misfortune of engendering a rather formidable opposition as a result of their adventure in Afghanistan. They had equally disappointing results in their efforts to set up a viable patronage system.

The Patronage System

The Soviet answer to American alignments and surrogate relationships was a patronage system of its own with Middle Eastern states, designed to establish dependency and common areas of endeavor. A great deal of money and effort was put into this project once the possibility of success became apparent. Ultimately, the Soviets became deeply preoccupied with grooming Mideast clients to offset U.S. advances, but most of their work in this field was disappointing in the long run.

Moscow's first major breakthrough in setting up patron-client relationships was with Egypt in the mid-1950s. It was more a matter of an opportunity falling into the Soviets' lap than the final culmination of careful planning. The United States had been unable to establish a fruitful dialogue with Nasser because it never really understood Egypt's problems with Israel and was unreceptive to requests for assistance from Cairo. In the end, Secretary of State Dulles's policy resulted in a rupture that forced Nasser into the arms of the Soviet Union. The weapons supply agreement of 1955 and the Soviet decision to finance the Aswan Dam project in 1956 were the initial steps in what was to become one of the closest relationships between a superpower and a major Middle Eastern state in the post-war era.

The Soviet-Egyptian connection continued to develop until it reached its zenith in 1970. The only drawback was Nasser's very negative attitude toward the Egyptian communists, but he never let this interfere with his relations with Moscow and made it clear that while he would not tolerate local communists he considered the Soviet Union a friend of Egypt. Moscow poured at least $7 billion into Egypt, and consistently supported Nasser in his wars with Israel and in numerous other ways. In return, the Soviets were gradually able to establish a substantial military position in Egypt, including air and naval bases and personnel in the form of advisors and technical assistants. It represented a major investment, a comprehensive working arrangement, a position of unusual strength, and a highly significant intrusion into the Arab "Southern Tier" of the Middle East.

The rise to power of Sadat after Nasser's death in September 1970 initiated a gradual change in Soviet-Egyptian relations.

Sadat had never regarded the U.S.S.R. as Egypt's natural friend and ally, and in time his preference for the United States became apparent. At first he left the ties with Moscow intact, concluding a Treaty of Friendship and Cooperation with the Soviet Union in May 1971. Yet at the very same time he was eliminating Ali Sabry and other pro-Soviet leftists from the political process, a step undoubtedly not well received in the Kremlin. At this stage the Soviets were anxious to avoid a breach with their major Middle Eastern client, whereas Sadat wanted to preserve Soviet support in his attempts to reach a satisfactory agreement with Israel on the occupied territories.

The inevitable deterioration in the Soviet-Egyptian connection began with Sadat's expulsion of the majority of the Soviet military advisors and technicians from Egypt on July 18, 1972, a move that brought an end to Soviet control of many of the air and naval bases in the country. Sadat said that the step was not designed to be hostile, but to lay the foundations of a different relationship. What he envisioned, however, was a more distant liaison in which the Soviets would continue to enjoy a privileged, albeit far less powerful, position in Egypt while Sadat would have the benefit of Soviet backing in his attempts to arrive at an acceptable political resolution of Egypt's differences with Israel.

From July 1972 to October 1973, Sadat was able to manipulate the Soviets in this way. In October 1972 they agreed to continue aid to Egypt, and after the 1973 war started they supplied enough antiaircraft missiles and other weaponry to allow Sadat to achieve his immediate objective of pushing the Israelis back from the Suez Canal. It is not altogether clear whether the patron or the client was in the stronger position in this relationship.

The Soviets cooperated with the United States in bringing the October War to an end and briefly participated in the peace process until after the abortive Geneva Conference of December 1973. Following that, they were effectively eliminated from any mediation role by Kissinger, who also drew Egypt closer to the

U.S. than ever before and thus helped to start the dismantling of the Moscow-Cairo connection. Sadat's relations with the Kremlin grew progressively worse, and finally in mid-March 1976 he abrogated the Soviet-Egyptian treaty. This concluded a patron-client relationship that had lasted more than twenty years, one that Moscow had regarded as its most important inroad in the Middle East political equation. Its passing, in many ways symbolic of the Soviet Union's declining influence in the area, called into question both the ultimate value of the patronage system as an instrument of national policy and the degree to which the investments involved brought commensurate rewards.

The Soviet Union did not, however, give up on the patronage approach after the break with Cairo. It sought to compensate for the loss by diversifying its regional relationships. Earlier in the 1970s the Soviets had moved in this direction by seeking new clients, mainly in the Arab world. Overtures were made to Iraq, Syria, Libya, Algeria, the PLO, and the two Yemens in particular.

A treaty similar to the one signed with Egypt in 1971 was concluded with Iraq on April 9, 1972, and committed the two countries to a loosely defined system of mutual defense and cooperation. Syria was persistently courted by the Kremlin as the potential leader of a new Soviet-sponsored front that would operate without Egypt. Although appreciative of Soviet aid and other gestures of good will, Syria avoided a treaty relationship throughout the 1970s. Moscow began to give economic and technical assistance to Libya as early as 1972. Arms accords followed in 1974 and 1975, and by 1977 Libya had become one of the U.S.S.R.'s major Arab clients. Algeria, which the Soviets had befriended in the 1960s in the last phase of the struggle against France and the early years of independence, was also courted during the 1970s, but the relationship was not especially close and later cooled. The PLO was a constant target, yet there were no formal agreements between Arafat and Moscow. The relationship was mainly on the publicity level, involving tactical advantages for both sides.

Soviet dealings with North and South Yemen were in certain respects predictable and in other ways unusual. The Kremlin had always supported the emerging Marxist regime in South Yemen, upon which it could always rely. It had to recognize, however, that the former British colony was very much on the periphery of Arab affairs and therefore a limited asset, despite its strategic location. In this respect, Moscow was open to any change in the political situation that might bring South Yemen more into the Arab mainstream. Such a shift appeared when tension developed between North and South Yemen in the latter part of 1978 and early 1979.[8] The two countries were in a state of war from February 24 to March 16, 1979, but at the end of this period an agreement was signed to resume the unification talks that had taken place in late 1976 and throughout much of 1977. This created a rupture in Saudi–North Yemeni relations that brought North Yemen closer to the U.S.S.R. than at any other time during the 1970s. Russian military and technical aid was given to the Sanaa government through an arms supply agreement concluded in 1980. These developments extended Soviet influence in southern Arabia and increased the overall usefulness of the connection with the Aden regime. In October 1979, Marxist South Yemen was admitted into the Warsaw Pact and a Soviet-South Yemeni Treaty of Friendship and Cooperation was signed.[9] While these events were transpiring, there was a temporary decline in American influence in North Yemen.

Related to what was going on in the two Yemens during the late 1970s was the situation in the Horn of Africa. The Soviets had supplied Somalia with armaments since the establishment of independence in 1960, and had sent military assistance to the Eritrean movement in Ethiopia, with which the Somali government sympathized. The relationship between the Soviets and Somalia became even closer after the leftist regime of Siad Barre took over in 1969, and the U.S.S.R. was given naval facilities at

8. Halliday, pp. 64–65.
9. Nimrod Novik, *Between Two Yemens*, Paper 11 (Tel Aviv: Center for Strategic Studies, 1980), pp. 16–18.

the strategically located port of Berbera. This advantageous position lasted until the mid-1970s, when Moscow relinquished the Somali connection in favor of a preferred liaison with Ethiopia.

The overthrow of Haile-Selassie and the establishment of a Marxist regime in Addis Ababa in 1974 paved the way to this reversal. Though the Somali government was also leftist, the Soviets decided in 1976 that Ethiopia was a more important ally in east Africa. In May 1977 the Soviets began arms shipments to the new regime, and on November 13 the Somalis broke off relations with the Soviet Union. War broke out between Somalia and Ethiopia over the Ogaden region in June. This entire episode was costly for the Soviets. On March 22–23, 1977, representatives of Somalia, Sudan, and the two Yemens had met at Taiz, North Yemen, to discuss their security interests in the region and to construct a common front against Ethiopia in the emerging Somali-Ethiopian conflict. Soviet support for Ethiopia not only strained relations between Moscow and these countries it had groomed with some care, but also put the Kremlin at odds with the small but strategically located state of Djibouti, which achieved independence on June 27, 1977, and with the Eritrean liberation movement. In supporting Ethiopia, the Soviet Union engendered a sense of alarm among the Red Sea coastal states, which identified themselves as Arab and were trying to liberate Eritrea and protect Djibouti from Ethiopia. The risks were considerable in terms of Soviet strategic advantage and the Soviet Union's credibility as a champion of oppressed and beleaguered peoples.

By the middle and late 1970s, Moscow's attempt to compensate for the defection of Egypt by bringing other Arab states into its patronage system had run into difficulty. Syria and Iraq, which the Soviets considered particularly important because of their socialist orientation and their importance in the Arab system, turned out to be less reliable than expected. Although there was never a rupture with either country comparable to that with Egypt, both made it clear that they intended to pursue their own foreign policies and would not tolerate interference in their internal affairs.

An important Soviet objective in the early 1970s was the promotion of coexistence between the Syrian and Iraqi Baath parties and the local communists in each country.[10] The Soviet Union concluded agreements with Syria and Iraq in 1972 and 1973, respectively, establishing "national fronts" that allowed communists to participate in government in a subordinate status. Though Moscow considered these accords a tactical success, the two Baathist regimes remained suspicious of the communist parties and kept them under a tight leash.

The national front arrangement was never tested in Syria, but in Iraq it ultimately led to a serious rupture. Relations between the Baath and the Iraqi Communist Party (ICP) became strained in 1977, and the communist were purged in 1978.[11] A number of ICP members were executed, and the subordinate role of the party was forcefully reaffirmed. The crackdown may have been partly triggered by the successful communist coup in Afghanistan that took place just at this time, but it was more significant as a demonstration of Iraq's determination to control its own internal politics.

In foreign policy also, Syria and Iraq had equally independent policies. Syria's intervention in Lebanon in 1976 was very disturbing to the Soviets.[12] Although Syria was considered a particularly important ally, Moscow wanted to preserve its relationship with the PLO and its best friend in the Lebanese political spectrum, Kamal Jumblatt. In deciding to support the Christian side in the civil war in the spring of 1976, Syria had in effect become an enemy of both. The Soviets objected and withheld arms from Syria for a period, but the relationship was restored

10. Carol R. Saivetz and Sylvia Woodby, *Soviet-Third World Relations* (Boulder, CO: Westview Press, 1985), p. 50.
11. Robert O. Freedman, *Soviet Policy in the Middle East since 1970,* 3rd ed. (New York: Praeger, 1982), pp. 358–59.
12. *Ibid.,* p. 240.

when Syria shifted its support back to the Muslim-Druze-PLO coalition the following year.

Moscow also tried to end the rivalry between Syria and Iraq as part of its general policy of promoting cordiality among its clients. It never made any progress, however, and had to keep its accords with both countries separate. Efforts to conclude a treaty with Syria were stepped up in the late 1970s to take advantage of Asad's increasingly isolated position in inter-Arab politics. Finally, a friendship and cooperation treaty was signed in October 1980, formalizing the relationship. Yet Syria remained altogether free of Soviet control. In 1980, for example, Asad tried to intimidate Jordan by stationing troops along the border without consulting Moscow. Similarly, in 1981, he deployed missiles in Lebanon's Biqa Valley before discussing the action with the Kremlin.[13] Syria may have been brought closer to the Soviet Union by the treaty, but its foreign policy decision-making remained as independent as ever.

There was also friction over foreign policy questions between the Soviet Union and Iraq in the late 1970s. Iraq began to emerge from its protracted isolation at this time and to assume a leadership role in inter-Arab politics. It took issue with Moscow over its support for the leftist Ethiopian regime of Mengistu Haile-Mariam against Somalia and the Eritrean rebels. This disagreement inclined Baghdad to assign a higher priority to building Iraq's image in the Arab world than to the Soviet connection. In February 1980, Saddam Hussein issued a Pan-Arab charter that called for an end to superpower influence in the Arab world and closer ties with France and other countries of western Europe.[14] This annoyed the Soviets, but they maintained and even tried to improve the relationship because of Iraq's importance in the patronage system. Indicative of this was Moscow's decision to back Baghdad in the Iran-Iraq war, after having shown some favor toward Iran in the beginning.

13. Patrick Seale, *Asad of Syria: The Struggle for the Middle East* (Berkeley and Los Angeles: University of California Press, 1988), p. 397.
14. Freedman, p. 392.

The U.S.S.R.'s ties to Syria and Iraq remained intact up to the mid-1980s, though they did not produce the anticipated results. Military aid continued in a sporadic and sometimes disappointing manner from the recipients' perspective, and lavish praise for these clients was forthcoming from Moscow on appropriate occasions, such as the tenth anniversary of the Soviet-Iraqi treaty.[15] Yet the Soviet Union was never really able to control its Arab friends, often vacillating between accepting the limited advantages of the patronage system and trying to use it to direct the course of events.[16] In the end, Moscow gave up on trying to form genuine alliances with Arab states, resigning itself to reaping whatever rewards might result from its economic and military aid programs.

The constantly changing structure of the Arab system often left the Kremlin off balance. In the midst of Soviet attempts to promote the anti-imperialist bloc idea among the more progressive Arab states in 1966–67, for example, radical and conservative states suddenly put aside their animosities and worked together to meet the impending challenge of Israel.[17] Similarly, the Iran-Iraq war altered established Arab alliances, estranging former friends and creating unlikely partnerships. This required a shift in Soviet strategy, but Moscow was uncertain how to deal with this blurring of the traditional radical-conservative dichotomy in inter-Arab politics.[18] The problem was not really resolved until Gorbachev revised the Soviet approach to Third World relationships by minimizing the significance of political orientation in reaching agreements with regional states.

The Soviets also had little success with the less important Arab countries. Qadhafi continued to be a recipient of Soviet support, but his erratic behavior made Libya a questionable asset from the Kremlin's point of view. Algeria gradually ceased to be a

15. Carol R. Saivetz, *The Soviet Union and the Gulf in the 1980s* (Boulder, CO: Westview Press, 1989), p. 40.

16. Raymond L. Garthoff, *Détente and Confrontation: American-Soviet Relations from Nixon to Reagan* (Washington, D.C.: Brookings Institution, 1985), p. 683.

17. Saivetz and Woodby, p. 47.   18. Saivetz, pp. 71–75.

real client, and North Yemen's relations with the Soviet Union could not really be considered part of the patronage system. Also Somalia had been lost, leaving only Ethiopia and South Yemen as relatively close but politically marginal partners in an area where Moscow had by the 1980s only a handful of friends.

The Soviet attempt to establish viable working relationships in the Middle East through the patronage system proved a difficult and in the long run virtually impossible task. Countries that became clients either remained so only temporarily and then severed their ties with Moscow, or showed themselves to be rather fickle and unreliable allies. They often exasperated the Soviets by picking fights with each other. The perennial friction between Syria and Iraq, sometimes dormant and at other times very active, represented one case of this kind. Syria was also unpredictable in its dealings with the various factions in Lebanon, and Iraq suddenly opted for a special role in inter-Arab politics that bore no relationship to its Soviet connection. The two Yemens had confusing "on again, off again" relations with each other, obstructing Russan attempts to establish a real security system in southern Arabia. Frequent unexpected developments of this kind worked against the U.S.S.R.'s constant efforts to construct a viable patronage system.

Another problem was that though the Soviet Union has been generally supportive of the Arabs in the conflict with Israel, Moscow has its own essentially different policy toward the whole problem. As Fred Halliday has pointed out, "while for the Arabs the Palestine issue is, at least officially, *the* central question in contemporary Middle East politics, this is not so for the Russians. They see the balance of East-West relations and the protection of Russian security as more important than local disputes, however volatile or agonizing the latter may be."[19] Beyond this, the Soviets do not oppose the existence of the

19. Halliday, p. 68.

Jewish state, which they helped to found, and have never given the Arabs, including Egypt, sufficient supplies of armaments to establish military superiority over Israel.

Particularly devastating was the impact of several impulsive Soviet moves in the Middle East on Moscow's patronage system. The way Somalia was handled, with all its repercussions in the Horn of Africa and Red Sea region, considerably undermined Soviet credibility. But the most serious error by far was Moscow's ill-fated adventure into Afghanistan, which left the Soviet patronage system and all the methods it involved in shambles and ultimately led to a profound reassessment of the Soviet Union's entire approach to the Middle East.

The Afghanistan Trap

The Soviet involvement in Afghanistan from the late 1970s to the withdrawal of Russian troops in 1989 represents the most dramatic and ultimately the most painful of Moscow's adventures in the Middle East since the end of World War II. A classic example of decision-making in which the global approach was allowed to almost completely obliterate regional considerations, it should stand as a lesson to both superpowers of the dangers inherent in any Mideast policy that fails to take into account the sociopolitical dynamics of the area.

Afghanistan is one of the most complex societies in the Middle East. It is highly mixed demographically. The major groups within its estimated population of more than fifteen million are the Dari- or Persian-speaking Afghans, known as Farsiwan, the Pushtuns, and the Tajiks. Minorities include the Baluch, Brahui, Turkoman, and Hazara (Mongolians).[20] Aside from this ethnolinguistic pluralism, Afghanistan is in many respects not really a nation in the usual sense, but a loosely knit

20. Henry S. Bradsher, *Afghanistan and the Soviet Union* (Durham, NC: Duke University Press, 1983), pp. 11-12; Louis Dupree, *Afghanistan* (Princeton, NJ: Princeton University Press, 1980), pp. 57, 66–74.

collection of 25,000 village-states.[21] Furthermore, no pan-Afghan institutions exist to make it possible for the central government to unify the country and maintain control over it. There is also a strong tendency among many elements of the population to oppose change of any kind and to hang onto the traditional and Islamic ways of thinking and doing things.

In the history of Afghanistan from the reign of Amir Abdul Rahman Khan (1880–1901) to the Saur (April) Revolution of 1978, the dominant theme is resistance to central authority and to modernization. Amir Abdul Rahman Khan was one of the first to rule over most of the country, though he did not significantly alter the sociopolitical system. King Amanullah Khan, who reigned from 1919 to 1929, made a genuine effort to modernize Afghanistan through such innovative programs as the secularization of law and the emancipation of women. These changes by the "socialist king," as he was known by some, as well as his attempts to provide the kind of leadership needed to establish the country's real independence, were not well received. In 1929 the regime was overthrown and the king fled to Rome.[22] This episode was only the beginning of what was to become a perennial Afghan rejection of modernization and centralization.

During the brief reign of King Mohammad Nadir Shah (1929–1933), a rather unsuccessful attempt was made to set up a working constitution. It was not until the latter part of his successor's rule that any significant progress was made in democratizing the country. King Mohammad Zahir Shah ascended the throne in 1933, but for twenty years political affairs were under the direction of his uncles in accordance with an established tradition relating to the succession of a young man of eighteen years.

In 1953, Mohammad Zahir Shah was finally in charge of the government. As was the case with all rulers in the post–World

21. Anthony Arnold, *Afghanistan: The Soviet Invasion in Perspective,* rev. ed. (Stanford, CA: Hoover Institution Press, 1985), p. 97.

22. J. Bruce Amstutz, *Afghanistan: The First Five Years of Soviet Occupation* (Washington, D.C.: National Defense University Press, 1986), p. 10.

War II era, his major aim was to strengthen the armed forces to the extent that the central government could contain tribal anarchy and establish an effective deterrent against Soviet attempts to set up some form of control or to annex territory, a fear that had existed in Afghanistan since the 1920s.[23] Another goal, one that remained constant in the postwar period, was the incorporation within Afghanistan of the Pushtun area on the other side of the Durand Line in Pakistan. The king's cousin, Mohammad Daoud Khan, who was prime minister from 1953 to 1963 and a powerful force in Afghan politics, was particularly interested in this claim. Indeed, he devoted more attention to it than most Afghans thought necessary, and he was accordingly obliged to resign in 1963.

During the last ten years of his reign, 1963–73, King Mohammad Zahir Shah made a concerted effort to move the country in a liberal direction. He appointed a constitutional committee in March 1963, and this quickly led to a protracted period of constitutional monarchy. During this time, there were four basic ideological positions within Afghanistan: the traditional opposition to change and preference for traditional culture and Islamic principles, a liberal affirmation of political modernization along Western lines, a synthesis of both that sought to combine adoption of Western techniques with tradition, and a Marxist-Leninist outlook that aspired to revolution and the establishment of a communist state.[24] Underlying the introduction of new political ideas, however, was the perennial reluctance of a largely illiterate and scattered peasantry to cooperate with or play any role in the modernization process, a factor that the communist government had to deal with after 1978.[25] The king consequently had difficulty in making the constitutional system work effectively, and on July 17, 1973, Daoud overthrew him and set up his own personal dictatorship. Mohammad Zahir Shah went into exile in Rome, as had Amanullah in 1929.

23. *Ibid.*, pp. 13, 21; Bradsher, p. 17.   24. Arnold, pp. 45 46.
25. Bradsher, p. 18.

Daoud's regime was overbearing, and the tactics it employed in keeping the country under control ultimately paved the way to the communist takeover in 1978. The democratic system the king had tried to establish ceased to exist. The constitution and civil liberties were suspended, and moderate and right-wing political parties were suppressed. Owing largely to Soviet pressure, however, the People's Democratic Party of Afghanistan (PDPA) was permitted to operate as a semilegal organization. But when Daoud rounded up PDPA leaders following the murder of one of their principal ideologues, Mir Akbar Khyber, in April 1978, he was overthrown by the communists and executed along with thirty members of his family. Indeed, throughout his five-year dictatorship he had been in a power struggle with this small but determined party, finally losing to them through circumstantial developments.[26]

From the end of World War II to the Saur Revolution in 1978, the successive Afghan governments and most of the people tried to avoid anything that would lead to Soviet control over the country. Following the British withdrawal from India and the partition of the subcontinent, only the United States had the power to block Soviet incursions into Afghanistan. This led to requests from Kabul in the late 1940s and the 1950s for American arms. These went unheeded owing to Washington's preference for a working relationship with Pakistan, which was at odds with Afghanistan over the Pushtunistan issue. Pakistan responded affirmatively to American overtures, joining the Baghdad Pact in 1955 and SEATO in 1956. In the context of these developments, the U.S. government and SEATO endorsed the Durand Line as the permanent border between Afghanistan and Pakistan, but the Soviets expressed sympathy with the Afghan position on the Pushtun question. This helped to polarize the politics of that particular region and to force Afghanistan into a closer relationship with the Soviet Union.

26. *Ibid.*, p. 74; Amstutz, p. 37; Arnold, pp. 59–66.

In 1955, Daoud, as prime minister, had opened talks with the Soviets on the subject of military aid, having negotiated an economic agreement with Moscow the previous year.[27] Afghanistan's reliance on the Soviet Union increased progressively during the rest of the decade with the result that between 1950 and 1959, U.S. assistance was only $148.3 million as opposed to $246.2 million in Soviet aid, and there was a nearly total Afghan dependence on the U.S.S.R. for arms, petroleum, and trade.[28]

By 1960 the United States had become alarmed by the mounting Soviet influence in Afghanistan. In the 1960s and early 1970s, American diplomats in Kabul warned of the increasing Russian military and economic penetration of the country, and an embassy memorandum in 1971 mentioned the "subversive effects" of Soviet training of many military officers who go to the U.S.S.R. for stints as long as six years."[29] The initial U.S. indifference to Afghanistan and Washington's later commitments to Pakistan at the expense of Afghan interests consigned the country to the kind of Soviet buildup most Afghans wanted to avoid.

The communist takeover in April 1978 was in many respects an accidental anomaly. The PDPA was founded in Kabul on January 1, 1965, and was in every respect an orthodox pro-Soviet Marxist-Leninist party. In June 1967, it split into two hostile factions: Khalq under Nur Mohammad Taraki, and Parcham led by Babrak Karmal. Though both were similar in ideology, they differed on political tactics and differed also in their ethnic makeup. The Khalqis were largely from the less privileged Pushtun population. Though many were residents of Kabul, they were mostly from provincial background. The Parchamis, by contrast, were principally Dari-speaking Afghans and represented more urban elements of Kabul origin. In numbers the Khalqis were larger, with a membership of about 2,500, whereas the Parchamis

27. Amstutz, p. 20; Bradsher, pp. 19–20, 22–23.
28. Amstutz, pp. 22–26; Arnold, p. 39.
29. Amstutz, pp. 29–30; Bradsher, p. 27.

numbered only 1,000 to 1,500. In any event, the semiclandestine PDPA had no more than 4,000 members out of a national population of over 15 million.[30]

The Soviets considered the PDPA an internal ally within Afghanistan, and were concerned by the Khlaq-Parcham split. Just nine months before the April revolution, they had succeeded in effecting a tenuous unification of the two antagonistic branches of the party, but it is unlikely that they had a direct hand in the coup itself.[31] They immediatedly backed the new government once it had taken over, though they had little control over the course of events that followed. Once the PDPA was in power, the two factions vied with each other for control. The Khalqis quickly got the upper hand and then conducted a purge of Parcham in June and July of 1978. Babrak Karmal, though a Soviet KGB agent, was forced into exile, and the country was dominated by Nur Mohammad Taraki as president and the even more powerful Hafizullah Amin, who forced Taraki to make him prime minister in March 1979.[32]

The new regime was extremely repressive and quickly engendered a virulent opposition.[33] The new flag introduced by Taraki was primarily red and similar to that of the Soviet Union. This alienated most segments of the population, as did the cruel and authoritarian way in which control was established and maintained. As early as late May 1978, Kabul law professor Dr. Syed Burhanuddin Rabbani had assumed leadership of a National Rescue Front composed of nine Islamic and anticommunist organizations. This was the beginning of what was to become a ubiquitous and ultimately uncontrollable opposition. In mid-March 1979, a popular uprising against Khalqi officials and their Soviet advisers broke out in Herat and was joined by elements of the local army garrison. In response to this, hundreds, or per-

30. Amstutz, pp. 30–31; Arnold, pp. 48–49, 52.
31. Bradsher, pp. 82–84.
32. Amstutz, pp. 32, 39; Arnold, p. 76.
33. Bradsher, pp. 89–91.

haps thousands, of additional Russian military personnel were brought into the country.[34] By June, three-quarters of Afghanistan's provinces were in revolt.[35]

The Soviets were deeply concerned by the unpopularity of the Taraki regime, and they were also troubled by Amin's purge of the relatively more pro-Soviet Parcham faction of the PDPA. Most distressing was their inability to control the Afghan government, and this became a major problem when a rift developed between Taraki and Amin. When Taraki tried unsuccessfully to have Amin assassinated on September 16, 1979, Amin assumed power and had the former president secretly murdered on October 6. At this point, the Kremlin decided on direct intervention in Afghan affairs.

Amin not only alienated the Afghan people more than his predecessor, but also wanted to reduce his dependence on the Soviet Union and thus refused to agree to Moscow's demands that he call for a massive Russian military intervention in Afghanistan. The decision to send in Soviet troops was made on the premise that it would not be too internationally disadvantageous, and it was carried out after three unsuccessful attempts to assassinate Amin between mid-September and mid-December 1979.[36]

Soviet policy at this stage was based on the belief that Amin's regime was on the verge of collapse, threatening the advantages the U.S.S.R. had gained through the revolution, and the fear that even if he did survive, his distrust of Moscow would lessen Soviet influence in the country.[37] Most intolerable, however, was the fact that Amin was widely regarded as anti-Islamic and had an extremely tarnished image in Afghanistan, discrediting the regime and the supportive role of the Kremlin. Late on December 24, 1979, Soviet airborne troops began arriving at Kabul airport, initiating a full-scale invasion. Amin, whom the Russians had

34. *Ibid.*, pp. 100–102.   35. Freedman, p. 377.
36. Amstutz, pp. 43–44.   37. *Ibid.*, 40–44.

never forgiven for the coup against Taraki, was deliberately killed by a Soviet death squad and Babrak Karmal was installed as president.[38]

This dramatic Soviet intervention in Afghanistan was thought at the time to be a necessary step to remove a leader who was at the same time jeopardizing the revolution and undermining Russian influence. Moscow considered Karmal far more reliable and was convinced that he would be much more acceptable to the Afghan people because of his relatively moderate political orientation. But his restoration of a version of the old flag did not make much of a favorable impression, and he never had popular acceptance comparable to that of Janos Kadar in Hungary.[39] In the final analysis, the Kremlin had simply replaced one communist government with another that it considered more trustworthy and useful.[40]

The Karmal regime made several efforts to reverse the deepening animosity of most Afghans toward the communist government.[41] Two immediate goals were to convince the public that Amin was responsible for all the problems that had arisen since the revolution, and to patch up the differences between Khalq and Parcham to create the impression of unity in the PDPA. Another was to play down the Soviet presence while building up the rather shattered Afghan army. A further aim was to release most political prisoners and work toward more popular domestic programs. There was also the intention of gradually increasing the extent of training programs in the Soviet Union to build up a cadre that would ensure the continuity of communist rule. In the long run, however, most of these plans were unsuccessful.

The shortcoming of the way the Soviets handled the new situation in Afghanistan was that it did not take into consideration or even recognize that a fundamental conflict of interests had arisen between the communist regime and the basic social

---

38. Bradsher, pp. 179–86.
40. Amstutz, p. 52.
39. *Ibid*, p. 227.
41. *Ibid.*, pp. 55–56.

forces in the country. As Henry Bradsher has put it succinctly, "Karmal, in a puppet position that gave him no choice, heeded Soviet advice in a way that the two previous PDPA presidents had not done. He adopted policies devised in Moscow, but they had an internal contradiction. They were intended to deemphasize but not actually deny the Communist nature of the regime in an effort to soften policies that had proven antagonistic to the Afghan people. But they were also intended to remake the country eventually in a way that would insure a Communist nature in Leninist control terms if not in theoretical Marxist economic terms."[42]

The increasingly tenuous position of the Karmal regime was related to two problems. The first was that the PDPA government had from the beginning tried to implement major changes in a country largely predisposed against innovation of any kind before laying the foundations of pervasive power. The second was that the introduction of 80,000 to 85,000 Soviet troops initially, increased to 100,000 in 1982 and later to between 115,000 and 120,000, created the worst possible image in Afghanistan—that of a Russian occupation force in control of the country. On top of that, Brezhnev was extremely inflexible about the commitment of the U.S.S.R. to the communist regime in Kabul, and never considered changing his policy to address the actual situation that was unfolding.

As a result, the mass alienation of the great majority of the Afghan people led to an increasingly unmanageable opposition. Attempts to suppress opposition by official terrorism only increased the determination of the people to overthrow the regime. There was virtually no way for the Soviets and the PDPA government to set up any kind of "popular front" in Afghanistan, no way to enlist the support of noncommunist elements as an interim measure before consolidating power.[43] An impossible impasse had been established between Karmal and his Soviet

42. Bradsher, p. 241.   43. *Ibid.*, p. 246.

supporters on the one hand and almost the entire population on the other.

Numerous resistance groups under different leaders came into being in the years following the Herat uprising. They were largely disunited, however, and had no concrete political programs. Often, these groups sprang out of the villages in a particular location or formed in parts of provinces or tribes. The only connecting link was a common desire to expel the Russians and preserve Islam and traditional Afghan culture.[44] By the end of 1983, perhaps as many as two hundred guerrilla bands were established in various specific locations throughout the country, but without much coordination.

Attempts at developing a more cohesive opposition began in 1981 with the formation of two Islamic-oriented coalitions, each made up of numerous organizations.[45] Ultimately, the most prominent of these was the neofundamentalist Islamic Party (Hizb-i-Islami), led by Gulbuddin Hekmatyar. Though the intention in forming these coalitions was to organize and unify the resistance movement, each group had its own platform, ranging from a preference for liberal democratic institutions to belief in a Khomeini-style Islamic state, and there was often considerable friction among the various leaders. So great a divergence in ideology and political goals will undoubtedly complicate the future reconstruction of Afghanistan. But it reflects the principal reality of a diversified country that is highly nonconformist, tribal, and traditional in orientation. Indeed, it was this very fact that confounded the Soviets and frustrated their efforts to maintain the communist government in power.

The attempts of the government troops and the Soviet army to establish control over Afghanistan by military force were made difficult and eventually impossible by the kind of guerrilla warfare carried on against them by the resistance. The rebels, entrenched in their mountain fastnesses, conducted endless hit-

44. Amstutz, p. 89.   45. Ibid., pp. 97–101.

and-run operations, taking refuge in the hills whenever they encountered superior strength they could not deal with effectively. The *mujahidin*, as the guerrillas came to be called, ambushed Soviet and Afghan army convoys on the highways by day and launched attacks against fortified posts at night. They also carried out periodic assassinations of Soviet personnel and local communist officials.[46] Soviet and government soldiers were not able to do more than maintain daytime control over the principal communications links, the larger cities, and certain strongly fortified positions. Aside from that, 80–90 percent of the country was controlled by the resistance during the daytime and virtually 100 percent at night.[47]

The increasing chaos that spread throughout the country in the 1970s led to a mass migration of Afghans to neighboring states. Over two million took refuge in Pakistan, and about one and a half million fled to Iran;[48] in the end there were as many as five million refugees all told. Since most of the rebel organizations were based in Peshawar, the Pakistani government began attempting in 1981 to bring some cohesion to the resistance. Pakistan officially recognized the three moderate groups and factions of the neofundamentalist coalition. These organizations then energetically sought to recruit the various guerrilla bands operating in Afghanistan, with the result that by 1982 almost all of them had affiliated with one of the Peshawar-based parties. These affiliations revealed a broad spectrum of structural and ideological loyalties, including personal, tribal, and ethnic allegiances on the structural level, and traditional, Islamic activist, nationalist, and noncommunist leftist commitments in the ideological sphere.[49]

By the end of 1984, there were about 200,000 armed men on each side.[50] But gradually the war began to turn against the

46. *Ibid.*, p. 152.   47. Arnold, p. 98.
48. *Ibid.*, pp. 116–17.
49. Amstutz, pp. 107–8, 119–21.
50. *Ibid.*, pp. 177, 180.

Afghan and Soviet armies, owing in part to the poor fighting ability of the Afghan army and the Soviet failure to find an effective way of dealing with the guerrillas' hit-and-run tactics. Gorbachev assumed power in March 1985, and despite the fact that he already had serious thoughts about pulling out of Afghanistan, efforts were made to gain the upper hand militarily. Though Russian troop levels never exceeded 120,000, after the December 1979 invasion the Soviets had engaged in extensive bombing, mining, and booby-trapping, as well as the destruction of entire villages. They also tried massive firepower and attacks on rebel sanctuaries and supply lines in neighboring countries, especially Pakistan, as a way of overwhelming the resistance. The United States responded by sending military aid to the insurgents, at an estimated cost level of $30 million in 1983, $120 million in 1984, $250 million in 1985, and $600 million annually after that until a much higher figure was reached near the end of the war.[51]

In 1985, the talented General Mikhail Zaitsev was put in charge of Soviet military operations in Afghanistan, reportedly with orders to start winning.[52] Zaitsev was briefly able to turn the military balance against the resistance through the use of special forces, by increased air attacks on civilian targets, and by applying military pressure on Pakistan in an attempt to obstruct arms supplies to the rebels.[53] But in 1986, when the United States started supplying the guerrillas with sophisticated Stinger antiaircraft missiles, the tide turned. Suddenly, the Soviets lost control of the air in areas where these highly effective weapons were deployed.[54] Encouraged by the advantages of American support, the guerrillas had by 1987 achieved greater unity and a

51. Don Oberdorfer, "Afghanistan: The Soviet Decision to Pull Out," *Washington Post*, April 17, 1988.
52. *Ibid.*
53. Zalmy Khalilzad, "How the Good Guys Won in Afghanistan," *Washington Post*, Outlook Section, February 12, 1989.
54. Oberdorfer, "The Soviet Decision to Pull Out,"

higher degree of military effectiveness, and were moving from defensive to offensive warfare.[55]

The decision of the Reagan administration in February 1986 to undertake a full-scale clandestine supply of advanced weaponry to the *mujahidin* initiated the first successful CIA operation to undermine a Soviet military intrusion into a Third World country.[56] It represented a break with past tradition and ultimately played a major role in the Soviet pullout. The transportation of $2 billion in sophisticated weapons, including Stingers and $1 billion in other supplies into Afghanistan, was the biggest operation of its kind since World War II. Most of the matériel was brought in from Pakistan on the backs of thousands of mules. Aside from the Stingers, other special war equipment included mine-clearing devices, helicopter-detecting sensors, multiple rocket launchers, and incendiary bullets. Together, all of these advanced weapons placed in the hands of dedicated and determined guerrillas made the Soviet and Afghan government military position in the country untenable.

The price for the Afghan resistance was very high. More than a million Afghans were killed in the prolonged struggle, as against only 15,000 Soviet dead. Beyond this, five million Afghan refugees, one-third of the prewar population of the country, were uprooted and living in makeshift camps just across the borders in Iran and Pakistan.[57] The resistance was divided politically and faced with the difficult task not only of ousting the communist government, but of reconstructing the country under a system acceptable to a majority of the people. But for most of the rebels, any price was worth paying to rid Afghanistan of the PDPA regime and the Soviet forces.

55. Anthony Davis, "Afghan Guerrilla Leader Builds Forces, Strategy," *Washington Post*, December 21, 1987.

56. David B. Ottaway, "What Is 'Afghan Lesson' for Superpowers? " *Washington Post*, February 12, 1989.

57. Richard M. Weintraub and James Rupert, "With Soviet Troops Finally Gone, Afghans Await Last Round of War," *Washington Post*, February 16, 1989.

As early as April 1985, Gorbachev and the Soviet Politburo had started a secret reassessment of the situation in Afghanistan with a view to possible future withdrawal. When Babrak Karmal resisted subsequent overtures from Moscow with respect to a phased pullout of Russian troops and a political settlement, he was replaced on May 4, 1986, with Dr. Najibullah.[58] From early 1985 until the decision was finally made to withdraw militarily from Afghanistan, the Soviets wavered between pursuing the war in an effort to win it and finding a way to pull out with minimal losses. The combination of extensive American support for the *mujahidin*, declining morale among the Afghan army and Soviet troops, and the difficulty of establishing control over the determined and increasingly effective guerrilla forces operating in mountainous terrain, eventually convinced Gorbachev that the best course was to get out.

Aside from the tenuous situation in which the Soviet military found itself in Afghanistan, a particularly important consideration with respect to the entire Russian involvement from the beginning was the negative image of the U.S.S.R. it had created in the Third World. The Soviets had always tried to promote the concept of an identity of interests between the Soviet Union and the formerly colonized peoples of Asia and Africa. This endeavor had never been very successful and was made virtually impossible by the existence of a Soviet military intervention in Afghanistan to support a highly unpopular regime that was at war with almost the entire country.

The Soviet Union's reassessment of its position in Afghanistan and throughout the Middle East will come under examination in the following section of this chapter. But it should be mentioned here that because of a failed policy, the Soviets for the first time since the end of World War II were forced by popular opposition to withdraw from a country that had been officially designated as having adopted a "socialist course."[59] Though the

58. Oberdorfer, "The Soviet Decision to Pull Out."
59. Michael Dobbs, "Afghan Pullout Marks Historic Reversal for Soviets," *Washington Post*, February 13, 1989.

U.S.S.R. evacuated northwestern Iran in 1946, eastern Austria in 1955, and a naval base in Porkkala, Finland, in 1955, none of these cases involved the kind of anticommunist uprising that unfolded so dramatically in Afghanistan. It was, therefore, a major setback and one that demanded a profound reexamination of Soviet Middle East policy.

The Soviets had allowed themselves to be drawn into what turned out to be an "Afghanistan trap" by overestimating the significance of a local communist takeover in a traditional country. The PDPA was a minuscule and for the most part unpopular political movement in the country. Its successful coup in 1978 was really an accident produced by a destabilized situation and the malaise that had evolved from the uncertainty of the modernization and liberalization programs instituted by King Mohammad Zahir Shah before Daoud's coup in 1973. This had been followed by Daoud's repressive dictatorship and his impulsive move against a leftist demonstration in honor of a PDPA ideologue, leading to his overthrow by the communists.

Yet the communist revolution did not in any way represent a mass movement, and the new regime almost immediately alienated the vast majority of the Afghan people. A popular resistance that became increasingly powerful was launched in the early years and in time nearly the entire country was at war with its government. For years the Kremlin was unable to look at the situation objectively, and undoubtedly one of the reasons for this was the relative lack of open exchange of ideas and opinions in the Soviet Union. Once Gorbachev came to power and initiated *glasnost* and *perestroika*, however, a more accurate appraisal of the Afghanistan dilemma became possible. In a fundamental sense, the problem was one of developing a regional approach to the prevailing sociopolitical equation in this neighboring Middle Eastern country that had gotten completely out of control in spite of a sizable Soviet military presence. But this had to be done in the context of a broad reassessment of the Soviet Union's relationship with the entire area and its governments and peoples.

Reassessment

In the early 1980s, two prominent Soviet foreign policy specialists, Evgeni Primakov and Karen Brutents, proposed a change in the Soviet approach to the Middle East based on greater flexibility.[60] In essence, they were advocating that the Kremlin abandon the quest for an "anti-imperialist" Mideast alliance, a concept that had dominated Soviet thinking for a generation. Though the only hint of a policy revision along these lines at the time was Moscow's noticeable lack of involvement in the Lebanese crisis of mid-1982, the Primakov-Brutents thesis became a guiding principle after Mikhail Gorbachev assumed power in March 1985. The "new thinking," as it was called, was initially implemented in dealing with the situation in Afghanistan, but was applied later to the entire Middle East.

Unlike other Soviet leaders before him, Gorbachev had never indicated his own personal commitment to the intervention and subsequent war in Afghanistan.[61] He strongly favored improved relations with all countries bordering the U.S.S.R., including Afghanistan, and thought the Soviet Union should combine greater freedom of expression internally with a policy designed to diminish international tensions. With specific regard to Afghanistan, he felt that the intervention had become a burden rather than an asset, and that it was complicating the task of addressing the U.S.S.R.'s formidable political and economic problems.

Though an attempt was made initially to win the war, Gorbachev adopted a different approach when it became clear that U.S. aid to the Afghan rebels, which was likely to increase with time, was making the Soviet military position untenable. On February 25, 1986, he told the 27th Soviet Party Congress that he wanted to bring the Russian forces back "in the nearest future,"

60. Lally Weymouth, "Could the Mideast's Next Kissinger Be a Russian?" *Washington Post*, Outlook Section, September 11, 1988.
61. Oberdorfer, "The Soviet Decision to Pull Out."

and that he had an agreement with the Kabul government on a "phased withdrawal."[62] Actually, Babrak Karmal took issue with the Soviets on this plan, leading to his replacement with Najibullah in May 1986.

By the end of 1986, Gorbachev began exploring acceptable terms for the withdrawal of Russian troops from Afghanistan. At first he insisted that the post-pullout government be based on a communist-*mujahidin* coalition, but he dropped this demand by late 1987 because of American, Pakistani, and rebel opposition.[63] Earlier in the year, Foreign Minister Eduard Shevardnadze and foreign policy advisor Anatoly Dobrynin had said that the with-drawal of Soviet troops was "feasible" and "not far off." The decision to withdraw during 1988 was made between April and July 1987, and on July 20 Gorbachev told Najibullah at the Kremlin: "I hope you are ready in 12 months because we will be leaving whether you are or not."[64]

Finally on April 14, 1988, agreement was reached at Geneva by the United States, the Soviet Union, Pakistan, and the Afghan government on the terms and conditions of the Soviet with-drawal from Afghanistan.[65] The agreement was based on four accords. One was a mutual pledge by the Afghan government and Pakistan not to interfere in each other's affairs. The second, a Soviet-American declaration on international guarantees, left the question of arms supplies to the respective sides ambiguous. The third was an Afghan-Pakistani accord on the voluntary re-turn of the five million refugees living in Pakistan and Iran. The fourth was an agreement signed by the four countries on the phased withdrawal of Soviet forces, to be completed by February 15, 1989.

The last Soviet troops, followed by Lieutenant General Boris

62. *Ibid.*
63. Khalidzad, "How the Good Guys Won in Afghanistan."
64. Oberdorfer, "The Soviet Decision to Pull Out."
65. David B. Ottaway, "Agreement on Afghanistan Signed in Geneva: Soviets Pledge Troop Pullout," *Washington Post*, April 15, 1988.

Gromov, left Afghanistan precisely on schedule, ending over nine years of occupation. Some 15,000 Russian soldiers had lost their lives, and the image of the U.S.S.R. in the Middle East and other parts of the Third World had been badly tarnished. The decision to withdraw was the result of a comprehensive and undoubtedly painful reassessment of Soviet policy toward the area, which had previously been dominated by the conviction that the security of the U.S.S.R. depended on military strength and the continuous expansion of Soviet-sponsored socialism in the world.[66] Gorbachev had called the Afghanistan adventure Moscow's "bleeding wound," and following the pullout the Soviet Communist Party newspaper, *Pravda*, came close to admitting that the invasion had been an error in judgment in the first place.[67]

In the immediate post-evacuation period, the main Soviet concern was to promote the least damaging political settlement possible within Afghanistan. The guerrilla leaders, meeting as a *shura* (consultative assembly) in Islamabad, Pakistan, in February 1989, were deeply divided over Shiite as opposed to Sunni representation in the deliberations on Afghanistan's future government, as well as over what kind of political system it should be. In a tentative compromise on February 18, 1989, Mohammad Nabi Mohammadi, a moderate, was nominated as president of the prospective government, and Ahmad Shah, a fundamentalist, was designated as acting prime minister.[68]

Throughout the remainder of 1989 and into 1990, the struggle between Najibullah and the *mujahidin* was stalemated, with mounting hostilities and no apparent winner. The staying power of Najibullah came as a surprise to many. Fortunately for him, the Soviets continued to send military aid in increasing amounts

66. Dobbs, "Afghan Pullout Marks Historic Reversal."
67. Michael Dobbs, "Soviets Complete Pullout from War in Afghanistan," *Washington Post*, February 16, 1989.
68. Associated Press, "Afghan Rebels Pick Leaders for an Interim Government," *Washington Post*, February 19, 1989.

to the Kabul government, whereas U.S. assistance to the
mujahidin was initially dropped. It was subsequently resumed
on a curtailed level, but in a makeshift fashion that often included a forwarding process in which Pakistani intelligence was
able to channel many of the supplies to the anti-Western guerrilla leader, Gulbuddin Hekmatyar.[69]

The Soviets have encouraged a coalition between Najibullah's
regime and the divided resistance movement operating under
the tenuous umbrella of the Afghan Interim Government (AIG).
Washington insisted at first on transferring power from Kabul to
the AIG, but later considered allowing elements of the Communist Party to participate in a future government if Najibullah's
clique were excluded. In 1990, the United States and the Soviet
Union were trying to formulate a broadly acceptable political
solution for Afghanistan based on power-sharing, but this was
interrupted by the Gulf crisis and the standoff remains unresolved. The stalemate has been unprofitable for both superpowers, but the instability and fluidity of the situation within
the country leaves the future highly unpredictable.

Gorbachev, anxious to avoid a destabilized situation that could
have adverse consequences for the Soviet Union, sought ways to
promote an acceptable resolution of the political turmoil in
Afghanistan. Just after the military evacuation, he sent a message to President George Bush asking for American help in
achieving a peaceful settlement, proposing an embargo on arms
to all factions, including the Najibullah regime.[70] Though the
Bush administration initially intended to send supplies to the
mujahidin until the communist government was overthrown,
Gorbachev later tried to steer events in a way that would ensure a
government in Kabul that the Soviet Union could live with, even
if it proved far less accommodating than Najibullah. This led

69. David B. Ottaway, "U.S. Reconsidering Policy on Afghanistan," *Washington Post*, November 24, 1989.
70. Michael Dobbs, "Soviets Ask U.S. Help in Afghanistan," *Washington
Post*, February 18, 1989.

him to propose a coalition government as a solution. Nothing came of this, and the continuing war between Najibullah and the *mujahidin* left the Soviet Union and the United States uncertain as to exactly what kind of policy to adopt.

The "new thinking" goes beyond Afghanistan. It involves a reassessment of Soviet Middle East policy in general, and of Moscow's dealings with the United States and the international community as well. After Gorbachev came to power in 1985, the formulation of policy for the area was placed in the hands of V. P. Polyakov, the highest Mideast foreign policy specialist, "new thinking" advocates Primakov and Brutents, and Alexander Zotov, an assistant of Brutents. Working closely with Gorbachev, these specialists gradually reconstructed the entire Soviet approach to this important neighboring region.

Soviet decision-making in the pre-Gorbachev era had been based to a certain extent on the interaction of divergent viewpoints on the higher levels, with some input from academic and institutional area specialists.[71] The critique offered by the area specialists created a degree of pressure on the leadership to demonstrate the efficacy of their policies. Yet in the final analysis, actual decisions were often reactive in that they tried to cope with unpredictable shifts in Middle East politics in whatever way seemed to involve the least cost and the greatest benefit. They also reflected the restrictive influence of the relatively doctrinaire orientation of the Brezhnev-Kosygin period.

The major themes of the new policy have been the extrication of the U.S.S.R. from the Afghanistan quagmire with the least possible damage, replacement of the anti-imperialist bloc tactic with a highly flexible system of establishing friendly relations with states of every political complexion, and the active participation of the Soviet Union in the settlement of regional conflicts, including major involvement in the Arab-Israeli peace process and the attempted resolution of the 1990 Gulf crisis. The

71. Saivetz and Woodby, pp. 181–85.

evacuation from Afghanistan was accomplished adroitly and without a counterproductive confrontation with the United States. The switch from the promotion of patron-client relationships with a select group of "radical" states to the use of wide-ranging overtures to all countries in the area has entailed subtle diplomacy developed over an extended period.

Diplomatic relations were established with the United Arab Emirates and Oman in 1985, with Qatar in 1988, and with Saudi Arabia in 1990. The Soviets also supported the Gulf Cooperation Council, especially during the shipping crisis of 1987–88, which improved their image among the conservative states considerably. Even more important has been an attempt to set up a normal exchange of ambassadors and missions with Israel.[72] A helpful gesture in this respect has been the increase in Jewish emigration from the Soviet Union. Though less than 1,000 in 1986, it rose to more than 20,000 in 1988[73] and had become nearly unrestricted by 1990. Soviet Jews have also been allowed to visit relatives in Israel.

Another aspect of the new policy has been a degree of curtailment in Soviet generosity with some of the radical clients, a move in line with Gorbachev's general downgrading of overtures to Third World countries. Arms supplies to Syria and Libya have been diminished in recent years, and Gorbachev made it clear to Asad that the Soviet Union does not intend to bring Syria up to military parity with Israel.[74] The change involves, above all, an alteration in bearing and demeanor, a discreetly conveyed message that the U.S.S.R. needs to protect its international interests by developing fresh approaches and priorities in the Middle East.

Involvement in the Arab-Israeli peace process and other endeavors to resolve regional conflicts is a top priority in the new

72. Weymouth, "Could the Mideast's Next Kissinger Be a Russian?"
73. David Remnick, "Soviet Tests 'New Thinking' in Mideast," *Washington Post*, November 21, 1988.
74. Carlyle Murphy, "Syria Urged to Stress Defense: Soviets Counseling Shift in Arms Plan," *Washington Post*, November 20, 1989.

Soviet policy toward the Middle East. Since the failure of the Two-Power Talks in 1969 and the adroit maneuvering by Kissinger that left Russia out of the American-sponsored post-1973 initiative, the Soviet Union has been on the periphery of the major developments in the quest for peace. The Brezhnev regime had felt that a reconvened Geneva conference would improve the Soviet Union's general position in the Middle East, but was unable to arrange such a conference. Gorbachev, on the other hand, is determined to change this situation radically. His principal aim in this connection is to reconvene an international conference designed to resolve the Arab-Israeli dispute, a second Geneva meeting that would pick up where the first one stopped without having accomplished anything in December 1973.

Though one aspect of the Soviet "new thinking" is the determination to move away from confrontation with the U.S. in the Middle East and to establish an American-Soviet partnership in the area,[75] it is also committed to a procedural principle based on the belief that the requirements of a real peace are a comprehensive approach, the establishment of a Palestinian state in the West Bank and Gaza, and provisions for mutual recognition and security.[76]

When Arafat visited Moscow in April 1988, Gorbachev told him that "The search for a solution to the Middle East problem should be based on negotiations . . . and not on armed force." He also said that "recognition of the State of Israel and account for its security interests . . . is a necessary element in the establishment of peace . . . in the region on the basis of international law."[77] The effort to reestablish diplomatic relations with Israel is another aspect of the same policy, but Moscow has indicated

75. Alan Colwell, "Soviets Trying to Become Team Player in Mideast," *New York Times International,* December 12, 1989.
76. Evgeni M. Primakov, "Soviet Policy toward the Arab-Israeli Conflict," *The Middle East: Ten Years after Camp David,* ed. William B. Quandt (Washington, D.C.: Brookings Institution, 1988), p. 388.
77. Weymouth, "Could the Mideast's Next Kissinger Be a Russian?"

that Israeli willingness to participate in an international peace conference is a requirement for the restoration of relations.[78]

Soviet moves to promote a second Geneva conference have been executed with extremely agile diplomacy. To buttress its own insistence that the PLO be involved in the negotiations, the Kremlin played an effective role in reconciling the differences between the mainstream Fatah contingent of the PLO and the radical factions. It also influenced Arafat to accept Security Council Resolutions 242 and 338 and recognize Israel's right to exist. This was done to give the PLO "the legitimacy they need to be a full partner in Middle East peacemaking."[79] When the Palestine National Council moved in this direction in its proclamation of an independent Palestinian state on November 15, 1988, First Deputy Foreign Minister Alexander Bessmertnykh, who replaced Shevardnadze as foreign minister in January 1991, issued a carefully balanced statement in which he called the declaration of independence "a major contribution to the process of a fair political settlement in the Middle East," but left the question of full Soviet diplomatic recognition unclear.[80] Without endorsing the Palestinian state directly, Bessmertnykh referred to the need for a Palestinian "fatherland" and spoke also of "reliable security" for Israel.[81] The purpose of this ambiguity was undoubtedly to reassure Israel and thereby further enhance the possibility of convening the conference. On January 10, 1990, however, the Soviets upgraded the PLO diplomatic mission in Moscow to the status of "the embassy of the state of Palestine in the Soviet Union."[82]

The Gorbachev regime also sought the resolution of other

78. David Remnick, "Soviets Endorse Palestinian Declaration: Statement Appears Short of Diplomatic Recognition," *Washington Post*, November 19, 1988.

79. Judith Kipper, "How Moscow Pushed the PLO Toward Peace," *Washington Post*, Outlook Section, December 18, 1988.

80. Remnick, "Soviets Endorse Palestinian Declaration."

81. Remnick, "Soviet Tests 'New Thinking' in Mideast."

82. David Remnick, "Soviets, PLO Upgrade Relations," *Washington Post*, January 11, 1990.

local conflicts in the Middle East. During the tension in the Persian Gulf generated by the Iran-Iraq war, the Soviets assumed a circumspect role. When the Kuwaiti request to Washington for the reflagging of Kuwait's tankers was refused, Moscow agreed to do so in a quiet but convincing manner.[83] The United States then agreed to permit the use of the American flag on Kuwaiti ships, but the perception that the U.S. had a somewhat uncertain and impulsive way of dealing with such situations created the impression that the Soviet Union might ultimately be the more effective of the two superpowers in preserving the regional balance of power in the heated politics of the Gulf. The Soviets were, in any event, trying to generate an appearance of themselves as potential mediators in the Iran-Iraq war.

The new Soviet approach to the Middle East is really part of a broader policy toward the Third World in general. There is a clear desire on the part of Gorbachev and his government to settle regional conflicts everywhere by accommodating divergent interests. According to Galia Golan, a specialist on Soviet Mideast policy at the Hebrew University, "The way Gorbachev is trying to balance interests in the Middle East is part of an overall strategy that you can find in his policies on Angola, Cambodia, China, the Pacific, the Persian Gulf, South America, Western Europe. All over, really. You don't have to have stars in your eyes to understand that the Soviets these days are after stability, quiet and reduced tensions."[84] It has been suggested that a major reason for this change was to take pressure off the troubled Soviet economy.[85]

In the Middle East, the Soviet Union's major aim in adopting a flexible posture and promoting the peaceful settlement of disputes seems to be the establishment of a stronger Soviet role in the area.[86] An important underlying motive, however, is to

83. Robert G. Neumann, "Moscow's New Role as Mideast Broker," *Washington Post*, Outlook Section, October 25, 1987.
84. Remnick, "Soviet Tests 'New Thinking' in Mideast."
85. Weymouth, "Could the Mideast's Next Kissinger Be a Russian?"
86. Neumann, "Moscow's New Role as Mideast Broker."

create an international image of the Soviet Union as having undergone a sweeping change in every sphere, ranging from greater political liberalization at home to a more mature, efficient, and responsible way of participating in the world community.[87] The two top priorities, then, are to establish a genuinely powerful Soviet position in the Middle East, and to move the Kremlin to the center of the Arab-Israeli peace negotiations. Special concerns underlie each priority.

The interest in strengthening the Soviet position in the Middle East stems in part from the need to compensate for the losses incurred by earlier policies. There is, however, an even more sensitive related issue: the fact that 45–50 million Soviet Muslims inhabit the Central Asian republics and parts of the Caucasus. The rise of ethnic separatism throughout the Soviet Union is one of the more serious problems Mikhail Gorbachev will have to face in coming years. The combination of a new awareness among Soviet Muslims of their Islamic and largely Turkish identity, the rise of Afghan- and Iranian-sponsored fundamentalism among them, and the many emotions and memories conjured up by the Soviet invasion of Afghanistan have created a delicate situation in the Soviet Union itself.[88]

Soviet Turkestan and the Caucasus are component parts of the Middle East that were incorporated into the Tsarist Empire during the nineteenth century. When the peoples in these areas tried to establish their independence during the 1917 revolution and the civil war that followed, they were prevented from doing so by force despite the Bolshevik offer of sovereignty to non-Russian nationalities. Eventually they became an integral part of the Soviet system, though they resisted assimilation more than any other ethnic group in the U.S.S.R.[89] They may have enjoyed a

87. Henry Grunwald, "Sorry, Comrades—You're in History's Dustbin Now," *Washington Post*, Outlook Section, November 27, 1988.

88. Allen Hetmanek, "The Mullahs vs. Moscow," *Washington Post*, Outlook Section, September 25, 1988.

89. David Remnick, "The Legacy of Mohammed Endures in the Land of Lenin: Islamic Culture Defies Soviet Assimilation," *Washington Post*, October 31, 1988.

better standard of living than most Muslims living in the neighboring Middle Eastern states, but they never really forgot their Islamic cultural ties. And now this underlying sense of an identity that is neither Soviet nor Russian has come to the surface in the context of a broader resurgence of Islamic symbolism all over the Middle East.

The center of Islamic agitation in the Soviet Union is in the Tajik Republic.[90] The Wahabbis, unrelated to the Arabian movement of the same name and strongly influenced by Afghan fundamentalists, are an activist Islamic group in Tajikistan. They advocate the establishment of an Islamic state comprising all of Central Asia, and have even called for a *jihad* (holy war) against the Soviet Union. Though the Tajik Republic is the center of this kind of activity, it has appeared in other parts of Turkestan. In Alma-Ata in Kazakhstan, for example, fundamentalists sparked anti-Russian riots in December 1986. Expressions of Islamic resistance to Soviet rule are also constantly encouraged by broadcasts from Iran in the Azerbaijani and Turkoman dialects of Turkish, as well as in Persian and Russian.

Most observers discount the possibility of an Islamic revolution in Soviet Central Asia, and the March 17, 1991, national referendum showed a strong preference among the Turkestan republics to remain in the Soviet Union. Nevertheless, renewed Islamic sentiment in the region remains a significant development. Soviet relations with and standing in the Middle East will have an important bearing on the way Moscow is able to deal with Islamic forces of dissent in the Tajik Republic and other parts of Turkestan. This is therefore a second but equally pressing reason for the fresh approaches to the Middle East currently being formulated and implemented in Moscow.

The other top priority in Soviet Middle East policy—moving the U.S.S.R. to the center of the Arab-Israeli peace process—has been probably the principal concern of Mideast policy-makers in

90. Hetmanek, "The Mullahs vs. Moscow."

Moscow in the past few years. An enormous amount of activity has been focused on it. During his trip to the Middle East in February 1989, Foreign Minister Eduard Shevardnadze emphasized the importance of convening an international conference to seek a resolution of the dispute.

Shevardnadze proposed the formation of a "preparatory body" made up of the five permanent members of the United Nations Security Council to set the machinery of the conference in motion.[91] He indicated a certain urgency in moving toward a settlement of the conflict, urging a collective effort to address Israel's concern over security and the Palestinian aspiration for a homeland as the fundamental parts of a peaceful resolution. He took issue with President Bush's suggestion that the Soviet Union should have only a "limited role" in the peace process, and he continued to press for a conference despite the determination of Bush and Secretary of State James Baker not to be "stampeded" into a new peace initiative.[92] Shevardnadze also informed the leaders of Egypt, Jordan, and the PLO in a public statement that he had been instrumental in securing the agreement of Syria's President Asad to participate in a future international conference on the Arab-Israeli dispute. He added, "The Soviet Union intends to encourage in every way any positive steps aimed at surmounting inter-Arab differences and uniting Arab countries, so that they would engage in a constructive dialogue on the Middle East settlement."[93]

The Gorbachev regime considers the international conference and the role it intends to play in it of paramount importance. This is because its new approach to the Middle East needs to be complemented by an image of the Soviet Union as a superpower

91. Associated Press, "Soviets Seek U.N. Parlay on Mideast," *Washington Post*, February 19, 1989.
92. Patrick E. Tyler, "Joint Peace Effort Needed in Mideast, Soviet Says," *Washington Post*, February 24, 1989.
93. Patrick E. Tyler, "Syria Reported Prepared to Join Peace Discussion: Move Seen as Achievement of Soviet's Visit," *Washington Post*, February 28, 1989.

with a stature comparable to that of the United States. Without this, the effort to build a strong Russian position in the Middle East will have a very limited potential. It seems likely, however, that Moscow will achieve its objectives in this respect.

All of these developments reflect the reality that the Soviet Union has completed a major reassessment of its Middle East policy. The "new thinking" has been established as the basis of a comprehensive global *and* regional approach, and it is being implemented with determination and finesse. The differences between the current way of dealing with the Middle East and the techniques employed by past regimes is remarkable. Clearly, Mikhail Gorbachev and his colleagues are breaking new ground through the flexibility and maturity of perspective they have brought to Soviet Mideast decision-making. Their policy is, in any event, clearly more effective than anything that has been attempted by the Kremlin since World War II. It has also helped immeasurably to offset the damage done to Soviet interests by the relatively narrow and doctrinaire tactics of the preceding regimes.

The 1990 Gulf crisis brought the Soviet Union to the center of major developments in the Middle East in a particularly dramatic way. By aligning with Bush as a principal protector of a "new world order" in the aftermath of Saddam Hussein's invasion of Kuwait, Gorbachev effectively terminated earlier attempts by the United States to keep the Soviet Union on the sidelines. This also virtually assured the inclusion of Moscow as a major participant in Arab-Israeli peace process.

The major uncertainty surrounding the future course of Soviet Middle East policy is how it will be affected by Gorbachev's recent retreat from progressive internal reform and his hard-line approach to secessionism in the Baltic and Caucasian republics. Considering the advantages that have attended the Soviet-American rapprochement in world politics, however, it seems likely that the "new thinking" will continue to be applied to Moscow's external relations, while a more conservative policy prevails in the handling of domestic affairs and the separatist tendencies in the dissident republics. The perpetuation of this dichotomy may depend in large part on the attitude toward it in Washington.

5   TRANSITION

THE United States and the Soviet Union have been rivals in the Middle East since 1945. Like "giants in Lilliput," they often found it difficult to understand the patterns of behavior that developed among the indigenous societies in the postwar years. When Gulliver decided on deference as the best way of dealing with the miniature people on whose island he had been stranded, he was really taking a calculated risk. In the end, he had to flee because his enemies among the Lilliputians hatched a successful plot against him. Though the analogy has only limited applicability to the superpower relationship to the Middle East, it is true that Washington and Moscow have frequently failed to anticipate reactions in the area to policies they formulated, and in this respect they have made a number of costly and counterproductive mistakes.

A major theme of this book has been that the United States and the Soviet Union have to employ a regional approach to the Middle East if they are to serve their interests in the area effectively. If they do not accurately assess the sociopolitical dynamics operative in the indigenous states, they automatically put themselves at the disadvantage of not knowing what kind of impact any action they undertake may have on the course of events. A major obstacle to understanding the Middle East has in both cases been a preoccupation with the global approach, with matching each other's relative position in the shifting regional equation. Even in situations where an evaluation of the regional predisposition has been the basis of action, as in the American intervention to assist the *mujahidin* in Afghanistan, the motivating stimulus has too often been the presence of a Soviet challenge.

As we enter the last decade of the twentieth century, a very different situation is emerging in the superpower relationship to the Middle East. A threshold has been crossed and a fresh set of realities has changed the rules of the game. The ending of the Cold War, the diminished strength of the Soviet Union, and a war in the Gulf involving the U.S. and other powers are among the major new developments. The policies of the past have become obsolete. The local states are stronger and more sophisticated, and the limitations of superpower prerogative have been demonstrated. The world is more interdependent, the structure of relationships has been altered, and a revised understanding of political dynamics has come into being. Middle East policymaking for the superpowers has therefore entered a new phase, one that requires greater finesse and a more profound comprehension of how the region functions.

Power and Prestige

The U.S. and the U.S.S.R. have had an image of themselves as far more powerful and prestigious than all other states or blocs in the world. In terms of raw military strength this may be true, but from a number of perspectives it has been at least partially an illusion. Superiority in numbers of troops, sophisticated warplanes, and nuclear weapons does not necessarily guarantee the ability of a superpower to impose its will on a weaker country. The American experience in Vietnam and the Soviet denouement in Afghanistan are striking examples of how a guerrilla resistance can prevail over a superpower attempting to dominate a vulnerable Third World country. Similarly, the image and influence of the United States and the Soviet Union, whether in connection with subordinate allies, neutral states, or adversaries, has rarely been as advantageous or overwhelming as assumed in Washington and Moscow.

As the superpowers go through the sometimes painful and

always difficult process of reassessing and reorienting their policies toward the Middle East, the whole question of the real meaning of power and prestige in a considerably altered international system will have to be carefully examined. If the Kremlin and the White House want to encourage or assure certain kinds of behavior in particular Middle Eastern states or to establish special relationships, they must decide whether power and prestige as such can achieve the desired ends. In many cases it is likely that endeavors to further the aspirations of regional countries would be more effective in winning their cooperation than arms transfers, alliances, or the political use of images.

While not denying the appeal to indigenous regimes of gaining the backing and advanced weaponry of a superpower, they would undoubtedly consider it more useful in the long run to have assistance in the attainment of basic national goals. The governing elites in the Middle East are ruling over developing societies in transition, and many of these governments have been unable on their own to produce the social, political, and economic results their constituents demand and deserve. For decades, the societies of the area have been disturbed by what they correctly perceived as the indifference of the superpowers and their inclination to manipulate local entities for particular advantages in a larger political arena. A change of attitude on such matters in Washington and Moscow would therefore have a powerful impact on the political psychology of the area.

The very nature of the Middle East—its transitional character and instability—gives it an elusive quality. The reality that it is undergoing a process of rapid change means that it is open to change. Radical alterations in the status quo are a fact of daily life in most places, and often many whose quality of life leaves much to be desired pin their hopes on some new but undefined sociopolitical order. It is this fluidity in the Middle East that in a subtle way presents the superpowers with the opportunity to promote mutually beneficial shifts in the existing structure.

Regional conflicts have been the most debilitating aspect of the Middle East political equation since the end of World War II. The Arab-Israeli dispute in particular has obstructed the nation-building process and transnational cooperation in the Arab world, as well as the evolution of political and economic viability in Israel. It used to be thought that the existence of a common enemy served as a catalyst to bring the Arab countries together. Nothing could be further from the truth. The struggle against Israel has divided the Arabs, polarized the political system that exists among them, and been partially responsible for preventing them from addressing their social, economic, and political problems in a constructive way. Similarly, though the interest in security that all Israelis share may seem to have brought them closer to each other, the issue of how to deal with the Palestinians and the neighboring Arab states has divided Israeli society more than any other single factor. If the superpowers, preferably acting together, can bring this disruptive conflict to a peaceful resolution, they will have performed an incomparable service for both sides.

Until recently, the U.S. and the U.S.S.R. have dealt with the conflict in terms of using it to achieve particular advantages, which only exacerbated and prolonged the problem. Washington has at times had difficulty in preserving a viable balance between its peace initiatives and its search for strategic consensus with selected surrogates. In the process of promoting a solution to the Arab-Israeli conflict, it has often given priority to its "special relationship" with Israel, thereby impeding its effectiveness as a peacemaker. If the United States is to play a really constructive role, it has to separate the Israeli surrogate connection from the peace process. It can continue to view Israel as a partner, but at the same time it must remain impartial as a mediator. The Soviet Union has demonstrated its willingness and ability to move toward a relatively neutral position for the sake of conflict resolution. The U.S. should therefore adopt a parallel course if it is to play an equally constructive part.

The importance of both superpowers participating in the quest for peace cannot be overestimated. It should be remembered that the United States has been an especially close friend of Israel, whereas the Soviet Union has identified itself with the interests and aspirations of the Arab states and the Palestinians. Even though these affiliations may now be undergoing considerable change, Washington is generally seen in the Middle East as relatively more pro-Israeli and Moscow as comparatively pro-Arab. These are only labels, yet they reflect the common beliefs of the indigenous people. For an international conference to have a nonpartisan appearance, therefore, it must necessarily include the U.S. and the U.S.S.R.

Constructive transformation of the Middle East is another goal the superpowers should try to promote. They can be most useful in helping to resolve regional conflicts. Other possible fields of endeavor include limitations on arms transfers, technological and economic assistance, the further development of trade relations, and the encouragement of greater democratization in the component states. Whatever the United States and the Soviet Union can do to encourage change on these levels would play an important part in the area's qualitative growth. Yet an essential prerequisite in the whole process will be an alteration in the way both superpowers establish and maintain relationships in the Middle East.

Power and prestige do not come from manipulation or the use of force. They are more realistically the product of prudent restraint and circumspection, of fair dealing and consideration of the needs, fears, and aspirations of other societies, as well as a determination to stand up for these qualities under pressure. A great nation that can create a convincing image of itself as a just arbiter and a champion of equity can wield more influence in the world than one that tries to overshadow or dominate weaker countries. The United States and the Soviet Union could increase their power and prestige in the Middle East by generating such an image of themselves.

Instead of concentrating on grooming surrogates or setting up "common front" alignment systems, they should at least experiment with establishing relationships with Middle Eastern countries based on mutual interest and mutual respect. This would not only bring about more enduring partnerships, but encourage open covenants and reduce the level of tension in the area. Both superpowers have in the past emphasized the global aspects of their patronage networks, often placing heavy demands on their clients and surrogates. The United States, for example, has in recent years tried to force Egypt and Saudi Arabia to adjust their foreign policies to American requirements, giving almost no consideration to the constraints placed on these countries by inter-Arab politics. Somewhat less pressure was applied to Israel and Pahlevi Iran, but they too were periodically asked to conform to some U.S.-imposed standard of behavior. Unsuccessful efforts were also made to induce King Hussein of Jordan to cooperate with American peace initiatives that he considered flawed or unbalanced.

Similarly, the Soviet Union has sought to influence the foreign policies of Syria, Iraq, Libya, South Yemen, and other states to suit some game plan of Moscow in the Middle East. A great deal of effort was focused on the attempt to create a regional "anti-imperialist" front. In the long run, however, most of these countries declined to offer full cooperation, believing as they did that the Kremlin was not paying adequate attention to their interests and problems. The adventure in Afghanistan was perhaps the most insensitive of all Soviet moves in the Middle East. Seemingly oblivious to the intense dislike of the great majority of Afghans for the communist regime, the U.S.S.R. went to the extent of invading the country and carrying on a war against the populace to keep an unpopular Marxist government in place. The repercussions of this episode were so profound that a total reassessment of Middle East policy was undertaken in Moscow, leading to the very different tactics of 1988 and after.

Should the self-centered narrowness of this kind of super-power approach to regional relationships give way to more mutually satisfactory arrangements, as currently appear to be in the making, the whole structure of international politics in the Middle East could be radically altered. Given the new awareness in Washington and Moscow that different circumstances now prevail in the area, it seems virtually certain that extensive revisions will be made. There is clear evidence that such a transition has already started. In view of the changes that are taking place on all levels, especially as a result of the 1990 Gulf crisis and the war with Iraq, the ability of each superpower to reorient itself in terms of a more circumspect regional approach will deterine the extent of relative advantage and disadvantage.

Redefining Interests

As the United States and the Soviet Union go through the process of redefining their respective interests in the Middle East, the first question that has to be raised is the relevance of ideology. Though ideological self-images have until recently played an important role in popular and official thinking in both countries, they seem to be giving way to an objective pragmatism that could be much more productive. In the Soviet Union, the rather rigid limitations of Marxist-Leninist interpretation have been gradually removed through the changes in outlook introduced by *glasnost* and *perestroika*. In the United States, the stereotyped attitudes toward communism and other creeds foreign to traditional American values have gradually been replaced by greater flexibility in the way international events are understood. This change in the U.S. has been due in part to the confusion and disenchantment brought on by the outcome of the war in Vietnam.

Although a new flexibility is apparent in the American view of the world situation, the transition is fluid in character and marked by periodic reverses. President Carter initially adopted a relatively moderate attitude toward the superpower rivalry, but after the Soviet invasion of Afghanistan he revised his stance considerably in the strong position he took on behalf of U.S.

interests in the Persian Gulf. President Reagan revived the Cold War picture of international affairs, referring to the U.S.S.R. as "the evil empire." Yet after Gorbachev came to power in 1985, he almost completely reversed his outlook, envisioning future co-operation between Washington and Moscow. President Bush, perhaps more circumspect in his approach, has indicated a gradualist policy in developing a mutually satisfactory working relationship with the Russians.

In the transitional period, which will probably last for years, there will be a degree of tension between the tendency by the superpowers to revert to traditional ideological positions and the desire to move toward a more pragmatic and less aggressive way of dealing with each other. This has not yet, however, altered the new thrust of Soviet policy, and the same will probably hold true of the United States. As the drift in the direction of pragmatism gathers momentum, both countries will begin to shape their Middle East policies more in terms of a regional approach to the area, one that includes cooperation with each other. Aside from the mutual agreement on détente, an earlier example of this approach was the Soviet-American cooperation in the 1987–1988 shipping crisis in the Persian Gulf, which prevented the episode from engendering a superpower confrontation. This should, in the long run, progressively reinforce the transition.

This change in perceptions of the world reflects the fact that ideology has to some degree become obsolete in international relations, including the Middle East. Despite periodic lapses into highly charged issue-oriented positions, such as those taken by the Khomeini regime in Iran, the Gush Emunim in Israel, and the radical factions of the PLO, there has been a tendency to divest political orientation of its popular myths in much of the area during the past two decades. The most notable example was the rise of a new pragmatism in Arab politics following the 1967 Arab-Israeli war.[1] Nasserism, Baathism, Khomeiniism, and

1. Alan R. Taylor, *The Arab Balance of Power* (Syracuse, NY: Syracuse University Press, 1982), pp. 49–72.

other ideologies of this type have in large measure lost their appeal, and have been replaced by an emphasis on finite goals and the gradual realization of major aspirations.

What this means in terms of superpower relations with the indigenous states and peoples is that political idealism will play a less important role in the designation of aims, the formulation of policy, and the building of alignments. In divesting themselves of some of the ideological rhetoric that accompanied past position statements, the superpowers will create a more relaxed atmosphere, a change in the established pattern with which the local actors are bound to feel more comfortable. Certainly the Arab world, which has been gradually adopting a pragmatic approach to global and regional politics since 1967, will welcome such a change.

An important second area of transitional readjustment that the superpowers will be undertaking in the coming years is a reexamination of ends and means. Often in the course of the Soviet-American rivalry, the preoccupation with the ideologically and politically polarized relationship itself was so intense that it precluded any thoughtful consideration of long-range goals. Both countries have important interests at stake in the Middle East, but these need to be looked at in terms of their intrinsic value rather than from a competitive perspective.

It has become easier for the superpowers to separate their bipolar competitive orientation from their way of relating to the indigenous states. It is important that they continue to do so, since the functional structure of international affairs appears to be undergoing major alterations. As the United States reconsiders its relationship with Egypt, for example, the questions that have to be answered are exactly why Egypt is important for American interests, what Egypt's own major problems and aspirations really are, and how a mutually reinforcing kind of partnership can be established. Similarly, Soviet policy-makers have to ask themselves in dealing with Afghanistan, for example, precisely what there is about Afghanistan that makes it important to them, what the Afghan people and their government are trying to achieve in the future, and how a relationship satisfactory to both sides can be set up.

Although the strategic value of any given country to either superpower may be important, this should not be allowed to overshadow other considerations. It is understood that guaranteed use of the Suez Canal is important to the United States and that the Soviet Union must have the right to send warships through the Turkish Straits. But there are other reasons for both countries to promote durable friendships with the regional states.

To use Washington's Egyptian connection again, Cairo exercises a considerable amount of influence in the Arab world, despite the rupture that followed the conclusion of peace with Israel in 1979. Working with Egypt in a constructive way that seeks to serve the interests of both nations, the United States could considerably improve its standing and leverage in the Arab sector. King Hussein of Jordan could also be extremely helpful if Washington were able to meet him halfway and avoid putting him in untenable positions. If Moscow establishes a reasonably friendly relationship with whatever government eventually comes to power in Afghanistan, it can keep its borders in that area secure and avoid undue hostility with this neighbor and the adjoining countries. These are the goals that both superpowers should be trying to achieve in the remaining years of the twentieth century. They can best be achieved by arrangements that strike an implicit balance between global and regional perspectives.

The selection of means to achieve these ends is as important as defining the aims themselves. The traditional method of pressuring weaker states to conform to the policies of the superpowers is at least to some extent obsolete. The new mode of international politics is more circumspect, and it is also more likely to succeed. The basic principle involved is that whatever course of action is taken, it should at least to some degree be as beneficial to the regional state or states involved as to the superpower launching the initiative. If this kind of approach is used, the goal will almost certainly be more easily achieved. The one exception to this rule would apply in cases where the regional power is aggressive or hostile in the formation of its own policies. When this occurs, firmness of some kind is undoubtedly indicated, as was the case with Iraq.

The redefinition of interests by the United States and the Soviet Union will logically lead to an overall reassessment of Middle East policy. This is unquestionably already going on in Washington and Moscow. Since decision-making is the key element in policy formulation, there are certain changes that should be effected in this process. One is to broaden the input, to make it more open and to involve nonofficial specialists in the analysis of problems and the selection of ways to overcome them.

Gorbachev brought younger and more perspicacious advisors like Primakov and Brutents into Soviet Middle East policymaking. The result was the "new thinking" and an extremely adroit reshaping of the Russian approach to the area. President Bush has indicated an interest in tapping more than the usual government sources in reaching decisions about how the United States should deal with a number of internal and external challenges. The Middle East, which is high on his agenda, should certainly not be an exception.

Final decisions will, of course, be made by the leadership in Washington and Moscow and their top advisors. But greater consultation with experienced foreign service officers and specialists outside of government is particularly advisable as a means of developing the regional approach to its full potential. State Department area experts and academicians should be included in policy planning sessions on a regular basis, providing a combination of new blood and fresh ideas on how to deal with a volatile and unsettled area.

For too long policy-making has been restricted to the higher official levels, which sometimes tend to view the world in terms of questionably accurate premises. A different perspective, though not necessarily more accurate itself, could at least provide the advantage of devising policy on the basis of comparative considerations. Also, the use of independent authorities from the private sector would help to offset the bureaucratic orientation of the decision-making establishment.

The 1990 crisis in the Gulf led to a major redefinition of superpower interests in the Middle East. The September 9 Helsinki summit established the construction of a "new world order" as a common aim and laid the foundation for long-term Soviet-American cooperation in the area. The principal objectives of this joint endeavor in the coming years should be to deter attempts at territorial revision by military force, and the promotion in every possible way of the just adjudication of regional disputes and the democratization of political processes throughout the Middle East. Though these tasks may have to be addressed at different times and in different ways, they remain component parts of the broader goal of stabilizing the region on a relatively permanent basis. The major uncertainties, as mentioned earlier, are the direction of the U.S. approach to the Arab-Israeli peace process following the war with Iraq, and the unlikely possibility of a change in Soviet Middle East policy that could be brought about by the recent conservative trend in Moscow.

Options and Constraints

In defining the options and constraints that determine the parameters within which Middle East policy is necessarily made, the United States and the Soviet Union will be dealing with certain constants and variables. In general, the constant factors cannot be altered, while those that are variable are open to change. The greatest freedom of movement lies in the field of outlook and the selection of alternatives.

The two principal constants are the emergence of a far more friendly but nevertheless competitive relationship between the two superpowers, and their recognition that cooperation is mutually beneficial. Though preoccupation with the struggle for a dominant position in the Middle East may have been diminished by the new appreciation of the advantages inherent in a regional approach, Soviet-American competition in all regions of the world will remain a permanent dimension of international relations in the foreseeable future. The rivalry has not disappeared; it has simply assumed a different form. In the coming years, it will probably be less related to military strength and strategic advantage, and manifest itself in the establishment of more genuine and abiding political and economic relationships with the regional states.

Henry Grunwald, the former American ambassador to Austria, has described the situation succinctly: "A benign, pragmatic and less ideologically driven Russia may actually present a greater challenge than the old, heavy-handed, crusading power which frightened people and was its own worst enemy." [2] For the United States, this challenge is immediate and imposing. The profound changes that appear to have taken place in Soviet Middle East policy as a result of the "new thinking" will undoubtedly enhance the U.S.S.R.'s position in the area. If Washington is unable to develop an equally imaginative and viable approach, President Bush's stated objectives in pursuing the war against Iraq and building the foundations of a new world order will be undermined. Failure to completely revise the general thrust of American policy toward the Arab-Israeli conflict will be particularly counterproductive.

The finesse and adroit circumspection with which the Russians are currently handling their dealings with the Middle East, including the way they are moving themselves to the center of the Arab-Israeli peace process, comprise the most effective strategy yet devised in Moscow. Though the indigenous states may be disturbed by the way the U.S.S.R. is handling secessionist

2. Henry Grunwald, "Sorry, Comrades—You're in History's Dustbin Now," *Washington Post*, Outlook Section, November 27, 1988.

trends in its own republics, they are at least aware that the Soviet Union has taken a new interest in regional concerns and has a relatively balanced approach to the Arab-Israeli conflict.

The rivalry has become more subtle and refined, calling for more astute game plans on the part of the superpowers. Though the orientation has changed, therefore, it remains a constant with which the United States has to deal in any countermeasures it adopts. Another factor is that earlier manifestations of the competition may periodically reoccur, creating a degree of global tension. Soviet-American relations have not suddenly become cooperative on a permanent basis, but they have been altered and appear to be heading in the direction of greater harmony.

The other constant is the need to preserve the spirit and letter of détente, and perhaps to make it more embracing and extensive. The United States and the Soviet Union have recognized for some time—certainly since the 1967 war in the case of the Middle East—that they cannot permit the competition between them to threaten global peace. They have tacitly agreed that their involvement in any region will not be allowed to produce a superpower confrontation and possible war. What this has meant in practice so far is that both countries have exercised restraint and moderation in handling the outbreak of hostilities in the Arab-Israeli conflict. But an even more cooperative relationship may be required by the circumstances currently evolving.

In order to establish a balance of interests and affiliations in the quest for a peaceful resolution of the Arab-Israeli conflict, the equal participation of both superpowers will be necessary. This will also make it easier for each of them to apply pressure to the side with which it is more identified. Given their common interest in a settlement, such collaboration is logical and in keeping with the new orientation of international politics. There are undoubtedly other fields in which bilateral Soviet-American endeavor in the Middle East may be in order, but these will become more evident after the major task of finding an answer to the Arab-Israeli dispute has been accomplished.

The variables in the transition include dislocations and policy positions or changes among the indigenous states and super-power attitudes toward the area, as well as their techniques of establishing regional relationships and dealing with local problems. There are a number of uncertainties in the Middle East political equation as of the early 1990s. These include Israel's attitude toward a negotiated settlement, the kind of role the Palestinians and the Arab states will play in the peace process, the continuity of the regime in Iran, the character of the future government in Afghanistan, and the aftermath of the 1991 Gulf war. The way developments unfold in each of these areas will determine to some extent the outcome of each relevant situation and the ability of the superpowers to influence the course of events.

If Israel and the PLO and the Arab states do not cooperate with the search for Middle East peace, a resolution of the conflict will become much more difficult. It could theoretically even lead to an attempt by Washington and Moscow to impose a settlement. In any event, the willingness of the directly involved parties to become positively involved in the process will determine super-power freedom of movement to a considerable extent. Inasmuch as the PLO and most Arab states have indicated a very affirmative attitude toward convening an international peace conference, the main difficulty will lie in getting a reluctant Israel to negotiate on substantive rather than procedural issues.

The policies of the Islamic government in Teheran and those of the future regime in Kabul will likewise set up certain limitations on the degree to which the U.S. and the U.S.S.R. can maneuver effectively in the area. Should Iran succeed in provoking a greater degree of nonconformism in Soviet Central Asia or in establishing an anti-Soviet Islamic government in Afghanistan, the repercussions could be extensive and add a new dimension to the political structure of the Middle East. Though the Soviets may have abandoned their earlier insistence that a coalition government be formed in Kabul, it is likely they would not accept a hostile regime and that the most they would tolerate is one that is basically neutral even if somewhat distant.

The regional settlement that follows the war between the U.S.-led coalition and Iraq will have even more far-reaching repercussions. The kind of Middle East order it produces will set the tone not only for state-to-state relations, but for the practice of domestic politics as well. Furthermore, it will determine the role of the superpowers as the guardians of the international political structure of the region. Aside from the establishment of a regional security system, a particularly difficult problem will be a stabilization of Iraq that addresses the unrest among the Shiites and the Kurds that surfaced after the war.

The other variables have to do with the superpowers themselves. The techniques used in conducting state-to-state affairs will play an important role in determining the way the local actors relate to the United States and the Soviet Union. The key factor will be the degree to which Washington and Moscow adopt a comprehensive regional approach that attaches as much importance to indigenous concerns as to broader questions of relative international standing and power. Should movement in this direction be substantial—as now seems to be the case—the whole structure of relationships between the superpowers and Middle Eastern countries could be radically altered. Many developments—some of them difficult to foresee at this stage—could flow from such a change. The most positive eventuality, however, would be the emergence of a climate of mutual trust and understanding between the superpowers and the regional actors. The benefits for all parties concerned that could be derived from such a situation are virtually unlimited.

The way in which the U.S. and the U.S.S.R. handle local problems, including regional disputes, sociopolitical disorder, and human needs of all kinds, is another important variable. The most visible endeavor in the near future will be the attempts to achieve a settlement of the Arab-Israeli dispute and to arrive at a satisfactory regional dispensation following the 1991 Gulf war.

Success in resolving the Arab-Israeli conflict will depend on the ability of the superpowers to work together harmoniously and to bring the opposing sides into constructive negotiations. It will require patience and finesse, and cautious maneuvering on all levels. The most difficult problem will be overcoming apprehension and resistance to compromise, especially in the case of the Israeli government. The durability of the postwar reconstruction in the Gulf and elsewhere will depend on the degree to which it addresses the underlying sources of regional disequilibrium.

Dealing with sociopolitical disorder is equally complicated. Since both superpowers are anxious to avoid appearing to intervene in the internal affairs of Middle Eastern countries, it iş difficult to counter domestic political malpractice in the indigenous states without exacerbating the situation even further. It is nevertheless important that the regional order put in place after the Gulf war include some incentives leading to greater democratization and a more equitable distribution of resources. In the final analysis, however, the initiative in achieving these goals must come from the Middle East states themselves.

As to the economic and military needs of Mideast states, both the United States and the Soviet Union have given extensive financial aid and military supplies to these countries for decades. It is not to be expected that this will stop now, but there may be changes in the way such help is given and the reasons for it. The Soviet Union has already curtailed its aid to some traditional recipients as an indication that it is moving away from enticement as a method of grooming clients. The U.S. may do the same in its aid programs to Israel, should the Jerusalem government seem disinclined to take part constructively in the peace process.

Military aid in general may be diminished as a matter of principle, as already indicated in the aftermath of the Gulf war, and other types of assistance will probably be given on the basis of merit and soundness. Regional disputes would certainly be diminished if the superpowers were to lower the transfer of arms to countries involved in conflict escalation. Similarly, economic aid aimed at improving the quality of life in the region, especially in underprivileged countries, would help to lessen sociopolitical tensions. Aid should continue to flow from Washington and Moscow, but with a sharper focus on constructive end results and the promotion of greater domestic and international harmony.

Finally, there is the question of what the parameters of U.S. and Soviet options and constraints actually are in terms of the current realities of international politics and the new trends that appear to be unfolding in superpower-regional relationships. In very general terms, it is reasonable to assume that neither country can or would be inclined to go back to the kind of Middle East policy-making they practiced during the first four decades of the postwar era. The regional approach is no longer an option; it is a necessity demanded by the prevailing circumstances. There appears to be a tacit awareness of this both in Washington and in Moscow. This is not to say that altered global perspectives will no longer apply, but that the regional dimension has become a stronger element in the equation and can no longer be ignored. This is the basic constraint and it is not possible to develop an effective policy toward the area without taking it into serious consideration.

The real options open to the United States and the Soviet Union are to explore ways of cooperating with each other to mutual advantage, especially in promoting a stable regional order, and to develop and refine an approach to the indigenous states that reflects a genuine interest in their welfare. Without exaggerating the relevance of the Gulliver in Lilliput analogy, it is possible to see a similarity in what ultimately happened to Swift's character and what the superpowers are faced with theoretically. Unable to work out a satisfactory modus vivendi with the inhabitants of Lilliput and Blefuscu, Gulliver finally had to leave the land of the miniature people altogether. This is not to suggest that the U.S. and the U.S.S.R. will simply have to abandon all their interests in the Middle East if they do not do certain things, but that their viability as interested external powers will be severely limited if they fail to arrive at a realistic appraisal of their actual options and constraints.

The 1990 Gulf crisis and the war that followed demonstrated in a very graphic way the ability of unresolved regional problems to disrupt the political equilibrium in the Middle East. The principal lesson to be learned from this is that the indigenous social forces are powerful, and that the grievances they experience cannot be ignored. The failure of the superpowers to fully grasp this in the past only aggravated the situation and ensured the kind of dislocation that took place in 1990–91. The magnitude of the crisis should be the best guarantee of a very different approach to the Middle East in Washington and Moscow.

SELECTED BIBLIOGRAPHY
INDEX

SELECTED BIBLIOGRAPHY

Agency for International Development. *U.S. Overseas Loans and Grants and Assistance from International Organizations: Obligations and Loan Authorizations, July 1, 1945–June 30, 1974.* Washington, D.C.: U.S. Government Printing Office, 1975.

Amstutz, J. Bruce. *Afghanistan: The First Five Years of Soviet Occupation.* Washington, D.C.: National Defense University Press, 1986.

Anderson, M. S. *The Eastern Question: A Study in International Relations.* New York: St. Martin's Press, 1966.

Arnold, Anthony. *Afghanistan: The Soviet Invasion in Perspective,* rev. ed. Stanford, CA: Hoover Institution Press, 1985.

Badeau, John. *The American Approach to the Arab World.* New York: Harper and Row, 1968.

Ball, George W. *Error and Betrayal in Lebanon: An Analysis of Israel's Invasion of Lebanon and the Implications for U.S.-Israeli Relations.* Washington, D.C.: Foundation for Middle East Peace, 1984.

Bill, James A. *The Eagle and the Lion: The Tragedy of American-Iranian Relations.* New Haven, CT: Yale University Press, 1988.

Bradsher, Henry S. *Afghanistan and the Soviet Union.* Durham, NC: Duke University Press, 1983.

Brandon, Henry. *The Retreat of American Power.* New York: Dell, 1973.

Brown, L. Carl. *International Politics and the Middle East: Old Rules, Dangerous Game.* Princeton, NJ: Princeton University Press, 1984.

Brzezinski, Zbigniew. *Power and Principle: Memoirs of the National Security Adviser, 1977–1981.* New York: Farrar, Straus, Giroux, 1983.

Carter, Jimmy. *The Blood of Abraham.* Boston, MA: Houghton Mifflin, 1985.

———. *Keeping Faith: Memoirs of a President.* New York: Bantam Books, 1982.

Cohen, Steven M. *Attitudes of American Jews toward Israel and Israelis.* New York: American Jewish Committee, 1983.

Copeland, Miles. *The Game of Nations: The Amorality of Power Politics.* New York: College Notes and Texts, Inc., 1969.

Department of State. *The Quest for Peace: Principal United States Public Statements and Related Documents on the Arab-Israeli Peace Process, 1967–1983.* Washington, D.C.: U.S. Government Printing Office, 1984.

Dowty, Alan. *Middle East Crisis: U.S. Decision-Making in 1958, 1970, and 1973.* Berkeley and Los Angeles: University of California Press, 1984.

Dupree, Louis. *Afghanistan.* Princeton, NJ: Princeton University Press, 1980.

Ennes, James M., Jr. *Assault on the Liberty: The True Story of an Israeli Attack on an American Intelligence Ship.* New York: Random House, 1979.

Ernst, Morris L. *So Far So Good.* New York: Harper and Brothers, 1948.

Eveland, Wilbur Crane. *Ropes of Sand: America's Failure in the Middle East.* New York: W. W. Norton, 1980.

Findley, Paul. *They Dare to Speak Out: People and Institutions Confront Israel's Lobby.* Westport, CT: Lawrence Hill, 1985.

Freedman, Robert O., ed. *The Middle East after the Israeli Invasion of Lebanon.* Syracuse, NY: Syracuse University Press, 1986.

_____. ed. *The Middle East since Camp David.* Boulder, CO: Westview Press, 1984.

_____. *Soviet Policy toward the Middle East since 1970,* 3rd ed. New York: Praeger, 1982.

Friedman, Thomas L. *From Beirut to Jerusalem.* New York: Farrar, Straus, Giroux, 1989.

Garthoff, Raymond L. *Détente and Confrontation: American-Soviet Relations from Nixon to Reagan.* Washington, D.C.: Brookings Institution, 1985.

Ghanayem, Ishaq I., and Alden H. Voth. *The Kissinger Legacy: American-Middle East Policy.* New York: Praeger, 1984.

Granin, Zvi. *Truman, American Jewry, and Israel, 1945–1948.* New York: Holmes and Meier, 1979.

Green, Stephen. *Taking Sides: America's Secret Relations with a Militant Israel.* New York: William Morrow, 1984.

Halliday, Fred. *Soviet Policy in the Arc of Crisis.* Washington, D.C.: Institute for Policy Studies, 1981.

Hurewitz, J. C. *Diplomacy in the Near and Middle East: A Documentary Record,* 2 vols. Princeton, NJ: Van Nostrand, 1956.

Khouri, Fred. *The Arab-Israeli Dilemma*, 3rd ed. Syracuse, NY: Syracuse University Press, 1985.

Kirk, George. *Survey of International Affairs, 1939–1946: The Middle East and the War*, ed. Arnold Toynbee. London: Royal Institute of International Affairs and Oxford University Press, 1953.

Laird, Melvin R., et al. *The Nixon Doctrine*. Washington, D.C.: American Enterprise Institute, 1972.

Lenczowski, George. *American Presidents and the Middle East*. Durham, NC: Duke University Press, 1990.

————. *The Middle East in World Affairs*, 4th ed. Ithaca, NY: Cornell University Press, 1980.

Lukacs, Yehuda, ed. *Documents on the Israeli-Palestinian Conflict, 1967–1983*. Cambridge: Cambridge University Press, 1984.

Marriott, J. A. R. *The Eastern Question: An Historical Study in European Diplomacy*. Oxford: Oxford University Press, 1940.

Memoirs by Harry S. Truman, 2 vols. New York: Doubleday, 1956.

Millis, Walter, and E. S. Duffield, eds. *The Forrestal Diaries*. New York: Viking Press, 1951.

Moore, John Norton, ed. *The Arab-Israeli Conflict: Readings and Documents*. Princeton, NJ: Princeton University Press, 1977.

Nixon, Richard M. *RN: The Memoirs of Richard Nixon*. New York: Grosset and Dunlap, 1978.

Novik, Nimrod. *Between Two Yemens*, Paper 11. Tel-Aviv: Center for Strategic Studies, 1980.

Pipes, Daniel. *In the Path of God: Islam and Political Power*. New York: Basic Books, 1983.

Polk, William R. *The United States and the Arab World*, 3rd ed. Cambridge, MA: Harvard University Press, 1975.

Quandt, William B. *Camp David: Peacemaking and Politics*. Washington, D.C.: Brookings Institution, 1986.

————, ed. *The Middle East: Ten Years after Camp David*. Washington, D.C.: Brookings Institution, 1988.

————. *Decade of Decisions: American Policy toward the Arab-Israeli Conflict, 1967–1976*. Berkeley and Los Angeles: University of California Press, 1977.

Reich, Bernard. *Quest for Peace: United States–Israeli Relations and the Arab-Israeli Conflict*. New Brunswick, NJ: Transaction Books, 1977.

Report of Congressional Committees Investigating the Iran-Contra Affair. Washington, D.C.: U.S. Government Printing Office, 1987.

Safran, Nadav. *From War to War: The Arab-Israeli Confrontation, 1948–1967*. New York: Pegasus, 1969.

Saivetz, Carol R. *The Soviet Union and the Gulf in the 1980s.* Boulder, CO: Westview Press, 1989.

Saivetz, Carol R., and Sylvia Woodby. *Soviet–Third World Relations.* Boulder, CO: Westview Press, 1985.

Sayegh, Fayez A., ed. *The Dynamics of Neutralism in the Arab World: A Symposium.* San Francisco: Chandler, 1964.

Sharabi, Hisham. *Palestine and Israel: The Lethal Dilemma.* New York: Pegasus, 1969.

Sheehan, Edward R. F. *The Arabs, Israelis, and Kissinger: A Secret History of American Diplomacy in the Middle East.* New York: Reader's Digest Press, 1976.

Spiegel, Steven L. *The Other Arab-Israeli Conflict: Making America's Middle East Policy, From Truman to Reagan.* Chicago: University of Chicago Press, 1985.

Taylor, Alan R. *The Arab Balance of Power.* Syracuse, NY: Syracuse University Press, 1982.

Tillman, Seth P. *The United States in the Middle East: Interests and Obstacles.* Bloomington, IN: Indiana University Press, 1982.

Tivnan, Edward. *The Lobby: Jewish Political Power and American Foreign Policy.* New York: Simon and Schuster, 1987.

Tschirgi, Dan. *The American Search for Mideast Peace.* New York: Praeger, 1989.

_____. *The Politics of Indecision: Origins and Implications of American Involvement with the Palestine Problem.* New York: Praeger, 1983.

Utechin, S. V. *Russian Political Thought: A Concise History.* New York: Praeger, 1963.

Vance, Cyrus. *Hard Choices: Critical Years in America's Foreign Policy.* New York: Simon and Schuster, 1983.

Williams, William Appleman. *The Tragedy of American Diplomacy.* New York: Dell, 1962.

INDEX

INDEX   211

CONTEMPORARY ISSUES
IN THE MIDDLE EAST

This well-established series continues to focus primarily on twentieth-century developments that have current impact and significance throughout the entire region, from North Africa to the borders of Central Asia.
Recent titles in the series include:

The Superpowers and the Middle East
was composed in 9.5 on 13 Trump Mediaeval on a
Merganthaler Linotron 202 by D&T Typesetting Service;
printed by sheet-fed offset on 60-pound acid-free
Glatfelter B-16 Natural, Smyth-sewn and bound over
binder's boards in Holliston Roxite B, and perfect bound
with paper covers printed in 2 colors by
McNaughton & Gunn Lithographers; designed by
Kachergis Book Design
and published by
SYRACUSE UNIVERSITY PRESS

Syracuse, New York 13244-5160